A BIG AND A LITTLE ONE IS GONE

P

A BIG AND A LITTLE ONE IS GONE

Crisis Therapy with a Two-year-old Boy

Elisabeth Cleve

KARNAC

Originally published in Swedish in 2002 as
En stor och en liten är borta. Kristerapi med en tvåårig pojke
by Wahlström & Widstrand

First published in 2008 by
Karnac Books Ltd
118 Finchley Road
London NW3 5HT

British Library Cataloguing in Publication Data

A C.I.P. for this book is available from the British Library

ISBN 978 1 85575 541 3

Translated by Inger B

Illustrations by the au

Edited, designed and
www.studiopublishir
e-mail: studio@publis

Printed and bound in   rfolk

10 9 8 7 6 5 4 3 2 1

www.karnacbooks.co.

CONTENTS

ACKNOWLEDGEMENTS

For many years now I have worked as a psychologist and psychotherapist for children and adolescents at the Erica Foundation in Stockholm. Throughout these years I have given psychotherapeutic treatment to a great number of boys and girls of all ages in difficult life situations. In most cases, they have needed psychological help for problems within their families, their own personal problems or traumatic events such as disease, divorce or death.

In this book I want to show how little children who have undergone a traumatic experience can benefit from psychotherapeutic treatment. The little patient whose story I am going to tell is named Victor. He is two and a half years old when he comes to the Erica Foundation with his father. He has just recently lost both his mother and his baby brother in a violent traffic accident.

I present Victor's crisis therapy as a documentary narrative. The psychic healing process is recounted exactly as it has taken place in the therapy room. Nothing has been omitted or altered to any essential degree. I have made the changes necessary to protect the privacy of Victor, his father, their family, and other people close to them. Victor is, of course, still too young to be able to understand the written text. However, I hope that in the future, when he starts to look back and wonder about his early years, this narrative will provide a piece of his history for him.

I would like to express my deep gratitude to Victor, who so clearly has shown me the strength and courage that a little child can possess in difficult times. I am also grateful to Victor's father, who so generously has given me permission to write this book. Thanks go also to the many other children whom I have met in similar situations. They have convinced me that psychotherapeutic treatment eases psychic pain after traumatic experiences.

I would also like to extend my gratitude to psychotherapist Jorge Maluenda, who has been responsible for the support talks with the parents of many of the children in my care. I gratefully acknowledge all the encouragement and support from my colleagues at the Erica Foundation. Of these I would like to give special mention to psychotherapists Britta Blomberg and Ewa Heller Ekblad, Associate Professor Gunnar Carlberg, Dr Sari Granström, chief psychiatrist at the Erica Foundation, and Dr Magnus Kihlbom, former chief psychiatrist. Further thanks go to psychotherapists Irène Nordgren and Anna Tydén, who, together with information specialist Thea Sterner, have assisted me by going over the manuscript.

An especially warm acknowledgment of gratitude goes to Professor Siv Boalt Boëthius, Director of the Erica Foundation. She has backed me in all the extra work it takes to write books about child psychotherapy and we have had a long and valuable collaboration.

I greatly appreciate the care and energy that Ingrid Boëthius-Kay and Pamela Boston have put into the translation of this book. Former editor Fran Newhouse and Ida Carlin have provided valuable editorial input.

Last but not least, I would like to thank my family: my daughters, Susanna and Catharina, for their genuine interest in my work and for insightful comments on the manuscript, and my husband, Egon, for his encouragement and patience.

Special words of appreciation from the author

I would like to extend warm words of appreciation to Angela and Per Boëthius of Gothenburg, Sweden, and to their family. Their generous donation has made it possible for me to write this book.

The donation comes from a memorial fund established by the Boëthius family to honour the memory of their daughter, Helena Boëthius, who was killed in a traffic accident in the summer of 2000. She left behind two children, a girl of seven and a boy who had just recently turned four. Both children survived the violent head-on collision.

The family have intended that donations from the memorial fund be used to deepen the knowledge of how little children in crisis can be helped. I hope that this book, which I have been entrusted to write, will serve this purpose.

Once again, thank you.

Ami Lönnroth[1]

What is a little child capable of understanding? This question inevitably comes to mind as we interact with the little children in our lives. We are amazed at their ability to recall events and people, and we laugh when they give us their own version of the well-meaning but sometimes nagging words of adults. The way they show their compassion for others astounds us. The question reaches a peak of importance when tragic events strike very young children. Can they understand? What can they understand? And what can they make of their knowledge if they have understood?

A little child who is dealt the hardest of blows that life can bring is the subject of this book. A two-year-old boy loses his mother and younger brother in a traffic accident. Now his life must go on together with his desperately grieving father. How is this possible?

"Hold my daddy's hand," chants little Victor in the middle of his play during his third therapy session with his therapist, Elisabeth Cleve. Dad, who waits outside the room, reaches for his handkerchief, touched to tears. This is one of the episodes in a deeply moving account of how a little boy learns to master a life situation that the grown-ups around him at first thought he understood nothing about.

With care and alertness, the therapist pilots Victor through fifteen therapy sessions. We as readers are fascinated by Victor's unbelievable capacity for working through all that has happened to him as well as by the care he shows his father in their shared loss. Step by step he approaches the finality of this loss, at last accepting it and absorbing it into his conscious life.

Elisabeth Cleve gives us a methodical account of the fifteen sessions she has with this little patient, interspersed with synopses of the talks that her male colleague has with the father. In one instance the little boy is sitting "like a mother who is cooing lovingly at her little guy. His facial expressions look like a mother's and his gestures are just like a mother's. He shows me, as he has done before, that he remembers exactly how his mother used to cuddle him." And when he takes the hands of his therapist and holds them against his chest, she puts words to what he feels: "Yes, she'll always be in there, in your heart. In there you'll remember. We always keep our finest memories in our hearts. That's good."

Moved and captivated, we get to experience time and again the strong moments in the interplay between the therapist and her little patient, who, after the above incident, thanks the therapist for helping him recollect the memory of his mother by saying, "Thank you, help to me."

What is it, then, that crisis therapy can give such a little child, which could not be given to him by his compassionate family and day-care teachers?

As I see it, the first and foremost factor is the deep respect for the individual, Victor. He is taken with the most profound seriousness. The therapist does not give into her impulse to let her own emotion come out in hugs and tenderness. Such a response would dilute the pain that the boy must be allowed to feel and work through in order to move on with his life.

Victor gets his very own space in therapy, which is not possible in a day-care setting. During therapy he can also let go of the responsibility he feels for his father and his other grieving relatives. This same feeling of responsibility made him react with exaggerated cheerfulness after the death of his mum and brother in order to make his dad happy again.

We also get overwhelming evidence in this book of the healing power of play. Sometimes Victor sets up a scene with wooden figures from the Pippi Longstocking story. After coming to sharp and stirring insights during a therapy session, Victor can feel quite simply compelled to end it with Pippi, "who always stays on top of things" and "who instils hope for an exciting life, even without brothers or sisters and with a mum away in heaven".

Victor lets his therapist know on several occasions when something in therapy makes him feel better. He understands how good it is that he and his dad can make each other feel better.

It is hard to see children suffer. We want to shield children from pain as much as possible. But often we actually increase their pain by not talking to them about it and by not listening to what they are trying to get across to us.

Elisabeth Cleve's book is an excellent guide to understanding a little child's many modes of expression. It is not hampered by obscure, specialized terminology and should be understandable and helpful to a parent or grandparent without a background in psychology as well as to school and day-care personnel and other professionals whose daily task is to help children meet and cope with life's difficulties.

Note

1. Ami Lönnroth is a Swedish journalist.

Monica Lanyado

When disaster strikes a family, it may make the headlines for a few days, gather much sympathy and compassion from all who know the family for a few weeks, but then, all too often, a social silence can descend in which no one knows any more how to help them or what to say or do to ease their unhappiness.

This remarkable book demonstrates the ways in which psychoanalytic psychotherapy, often mistakenly thought to be only a rather inflexible, long-term treatment, can in fact be adapted through "crisis therapy" to significantly help a father and his very young son in a clearly time-limited way.

"Fredrik" is persuaded by his family to seek help for his two-and-a-half-year-old son, "Victor", following a tragic traffic accident in which Victor's mother and baby brother were killed. Although Victor survived the crash without injury, he has not spoken about it at all and, two months on from the accident, seems determined to be overactive and cheerful with all the distressed adults around him. They all wonder how much he understands about what has happened and what can be considered to be a "normal" two-and-a-half-year-old response to such a terrible situation.

They turn for help to the Erica Foundation in Stockholm, an internationally highly respected psychoanalytical clinic and training institution for children and their families. There is a fine tradition of psychoanalytic work in this beautiful old building, with all its stairs and carefully thought out treatment spaces, dating back to the 1930s. We get a keen sense of this in Cleve's book, together with the changing Scandinavian seasons, from the depths of icy winter when Fredrik and Victor first come for treatment through to the following summer when the crisis therapy comes to an end. The coldness and bleakness of their terrible loss at the start of their treatment, and the cautious resurgence of a liveliness and warmth by the end of it, mirror the seasons.

Cleve and her colleague Jorge, who works with Fredrik, offer the depleted family, in which "a big and a little one is gone", fifteen consultations of crisis therapy. Their strong feelings about the suffering of their patients are vividly conveyed, as is the way in which they support each other. The reader gets a privileged and detailed account of this young child's sessions, giving deep insight into the ways in which he has defended himself against unbearable grief by his bright and cheerful behaviour. It is not until his final session that he is able to speak about his dead mother and brother. Cleve's therapeutic skill lies in her intense efforts to help him to face this terrible reality without becoming totally overwhelmed by it. She shares her thinking about this careful balancing act with the reader in an honest, open, and moving way.

This book is a study in childhood bereavement as well as a valuable account of the kind of psychoanalytically informed brief therapy that can be highly effective when offered in a timely, well-supported, and carefully thought out way. For both of these reasons, it is an unusual and valuable resource to clinicians.

There is always room for other clinicians reading such a detailed account to disagree with the author's clinical technique and conclusions, and it is important to remember that psychoanalytic work differs according to its history in each country in which it has taken root. The value of clinical accounts such as these is the discussions that it raises of these important issues and, above all, the recognition that there are many different ways in which psychoanalytic clinicians help their patients. There is no "absolute", no totally right or totally wrong way. In my view, much depends on the authenticity with which the clinician engages as a professional and as a human being with those that seek his or her help.

In this book we have a courageous and heartfelt example of what goes on between a therapist and her very young patient as they try to work together towards recovery from one of the most painful and traumatic experiences that any of us can imagine.

Introduction

A task for the child psychologist

A Big and a Little One is Gone is the true story of Victor, who, at two and a half years of age, loses his mother and baby brother in a traffic accident. Two and a half months later, he comes to the Erica Foundation in Stockholm with his father Fredrik, who has been advised to seek psychological help for his son. Concerned relatives, themselves in deep mourning, and the personnel at Victor's day-care centre, are all worried about how Victor really feels deep inside.

Fredrik has received professional help since the accident through weekly talks with a nurse. Victor, who was a happy and capable little boy before the tragedy, has now become even more "happy" and even more capable. He is eager to please and to be helpful, and is wound up all the time. He does not want to talk about the inconceivable catastrophe that has struck his family or to hear anything about it.

After an initial visit, Victor's contact with Erica Foundation begins with my psychological assessment of him. The next step is that we suggest a treatment called "time-limited crisis therapy" for Victor, plus support sessions for his father. We are two psychotherapists who meet with the father and son. Victor comes to me, and his dad to Jorge. The treatment is to consist of fifteen sessions, one per week for a period of three months.

In this book, the reader gets an opportunity to follow the psychological work session by session, from both perspectives, the little patient's and the therapist's. The content of each session is described in a concrete and detailed manner. I hope thus to show how the psychological process of working through grief can take shape in a little child. It is possible to partake of Victor's hard struggle to find new ways to relate to the strange reality in which he suddenly finds himself.

An important task when helping people in such a traumatized emotional state as Victor and his father is to inspire in them confidence and hope for the future. Crisis therapy can be the first link to a new future. No matter how dark everything seems, life does go on! The story of Victor shows how essential it is to observe children's reactions when they are going through grief. It also shows the importance of seeking help after a traumatic event. Psychological help eases inner suffering and prevents future pain.

During the 1990s there were efforts to increase the availability of crisis and catastrophe treatment centres in Sweden. People of different professions, e.g., psychologists, therapists, physicians, clergy, and social workers, have been trained in how to deal with people in crisis. The idea is that all these professionals should be able to assist people who have been struck by some form of catastrophe. It is well known that a person in shock needs not only physical but also psychological help as soon as possible. A person in crisis may need professional psychotherapeutic help. If such is the case, crisis therapy can be a suitable treatment method for both adults and children of all ages. Methods have been developed primarily to help adults and school-age children, but not very young children.

It is often said that "the younger children are when they suffer a great loss, the sooner they forget". But how can we expect a child to forget a parent or a sibling? My experience tells me instead that if a child is too young to remember with his brain, traumatic memories will lodge themselves in his body and soul. Such memories can then be the root of both physical and psychic symptoms.

Not very long ago it was commonly considered wrong to talk to little children about a dear one who had died. Doing so was thought to intensify their sense of loss and distress. This view has affected many people who lost someone dear to them during their childhood. The result has been that, as adults, they recount how abandoned they felt in their sorrow and how they had to manage alone. It was not the death in itself, however much of a catastrophe it was, but the lack of help afterwards that gave them the deepest scars.

Unresolved grief reactions in children can become a hindrance to their future development. In the process of crisis therapy, a child can be helped to gain access to the psychological tools needed to cope with overwhelming feelings of pain, sorrow and unreality. In crisis therapy work, we focus on the catastrophic event that caused the crisis reactions. This work must be done in small doses. The therapist must be sensitive and receptive, both a good listener and someone who is ready to interact when necessary. A little child who finds himself in shock must never be forced to open up the emotional experiences inside him. The child needs to be both led and followed through his mourning process with great care.

One intention in telling this story is to show that little children can benefit from crisis therapy. It is important that such a treatment leads not only to an acute easing of the symptoms, but also to a sustainable lessening of the psychic suffering. A condition for offering a child such a treatment is that his ordinary daily needs are being as well taken care of as possible. Crisis therapy can never be seen as anything else than a complement to basic daily care.

After completed therapy, a child always needs to continue working through his grief together with one or more of the adults who are close to him. It is to be hoped that the child, while in therapy, will adopt a variety of psychological coping mechanisms. These should help him and ease his suffering in his new reality. When treatment is over, the child can continue to use these mechanisms. It is also generally less painful for adults to comfort and support a child whose suffering is not as profound as it was earlier.

At the Erica Foundation, work with children and their parents is grounded in psychoanalytical theories. These theoretical approaches are the basis for the treatment received by Victor and his father. Even though the focus of the book is on Victor, I want to stress that we always treat children and parents simultaneously, never just the child alone. Such is also the case for Victor's father,

Fredrik. His support sessions come to be very meaningful for him, but also highly important for his son. Short summaries of Fredrik's talks with Jorge during the time Victor and I are together in the playroom are presented.

By describing Victor's untiring work in therapy, I hope to impart a deeper understanding of the state of the mind of a little child who has experienced a great loss. It is my desire that the story of Victor will give hope and courage to those who are trying to provide help for children in similar situations. Personal courage is necessary for such a task. Victor gave that to me.

Elisabeth Cleve
Stockholm, September 2007

CHAPTER ONE

It started with a phone call

One afternoon in the beginning of March our secretary answers a young man's telephone call. At the outset, she cannot understand what he is trying to say. The man is desperate and seems to be in a state of shock. The words are tumbling out of him. The secretary realizes that it would be risky to tell him to call back at the proper time for making appointments. She is afraid that he will hang up, so she asks him a few questions. This helps him focus his thoughts. He tells her briefly about the catastrophe that has befallen him:

"Car accident . . . wife and baby dead . . . alone with little son . . . they say I should call you . . . gave me a piece of paper with your phone number . . . my son is two years old . . . don't know what to do . . ."

Suddenly he wants to end the conversation, and the secretary hurries to ask for his name and a telephone number where he can be reached. He gives his name, Fredrik, and a mobile telephone number. She asks him to repeat the number to be sure she has understood him correctly. She finishes the conversation by confirming for him that he has reached the Erica Foundation and that he will get a return call as soon as possible.

Shortly thereafter, the secretary comes into the staff room. She is visibly shaken and holds up the note with the information from the phone call. She reads us the note and pleads, "Help them if you can!"

We are all moved by our secretary's words and after a short reflection a lively discussion breaks out. We ask ourselves if it would be possible to help this young father and his little son. We know we have the knowledge and experience to ease their suffering. We have, however, an increasingly heavy workload and a constant lack of time. The number of parents who seek our help has grown. Unfortunately, we do not have resources to set aside for emergency treatment. At the same time, we cannot put this father and son on our waiting list. They need help immediately. NOW! This is a difficult dilemma. It should not be a problem to want to help right away, when such a catastrophe has hit a family. We also know that the faster a child receives help after a trauma, the shorter the treatment time required and the better the result.

After all is said and done, Jorge and I decide to ask Fredrik to come in together with his son. Somehow we will create space for them, both physical and psychological. It simply has to be possible. That two colleagues work together on a case like this one is a matter of course. We know that it will be mentally demanding and that we will need the support of each other. Jorge and I often take care of families together. He usually meets with the parents and I with the children.

I dial the phone number we have been given. I am ready to offer the young father an appointment time. Almost before the first ring, he answers with his name, Fredrik. He seems to have been prepared to pounce on the phone in a split second. I introduce myself and explain that I am calling from the Erica Foundation where we received a call from him earlier today. It takes a few moments for him to remember that particular phone call because he has made many calls after that one. He gathers himself together quickly and thanks me, but does not quite know what he should ask for. Other people can be heard in the background, encouraging him to say, "Victor needs help. He's so little. He doesn't have a clue about what's happened."

I tell Fredrik that I can hear what is being said and that I want to offer him and his son a time for a first visit to us. We want to find out if we can help them. I give them a time on the following day. Fredrik says neither yes nor no. I ask him to get a pen and paper to note the time, the address and our names. Fredrik does not answer, so I ask him if there is someone else who can write down the information.

A man who introduces himself as Victor's grandfather takes over the phone. He has overheard the conversation and knows where and when his son and grandson are to come. He thanks me several times and reads back what he has written down, "Fredrik and Victor have an appointment with Jorge and Elisabeth at the Erica Foundation tomorrow at 3 p.m."

I ask if they have far to travel and if they can find the way to our institute. Fredrik comes back to the phone and gives me his address. He estimates the distance from his home to our institute to be around five kilometres. He tells me that since the accident he cannot bear the thought of taking either the bus or the subway, so he puts his son in a stroller and walks wherever he needs to go. He does not mind the long walks because he cannot endure being at home for long stretches of time. He says it feels as if the walls are about to cave in on him.

Our plans for their first visit are to meet father and son exactly where they are in their sorrow. We will receive them and offer a space where they can express themselves as they wish and are able to, each in his own way. We will listen to what is said with words and observe what is communicated without words. I will concentrate mostly on Victor and get a sense of his psychic condition. Can it really be, as the family seems to fear, that Victor does not realize what has happened? Jorge will focus primarily on Fredrik.

We have two rooms at our disposal. We will wait to see what Victor wants. He can decide if he wants to be with his dad for the whole time or not. The rooms are adjacent and on the top floor in a beautiful, ornate old building. Many flights of winding stairways lead up there from the waiting room, which is on the street level just inside the entrance. There is no lift.

The one room has easy chairs placed around a table and lends itself well to conversations between adults. In the other room, in addition to easy chairs, there are different kinds of play material for children. In the middle of the floor there are two sand trays on a wooden base, one with dry sand, and one with wet. Next to these is a cupboard with a set of toys for children to use in setting up their own world in the sand. There are cars and trains, dolls and animals, houses and small home interior pieces, trees and fences, cowboys and Indians, and some other toys.

Other materials in the room include plasticine, drawing pads, crayons, magic markers, paintbrushes and paint. In a closet there are boxes with somewhat larger toy animals. In preparing to meet Victor, I also take out a box of wooden dolls representing people of various sizes and ages. The dolls are not readily breakable, and are easy for little children to handle and arrange.

We have considerably fewer toys than most children have at home. In a psychotherapy room, a child must be given a chance to work with his inner experiences. Too many distracting objects can make it harder for the child to get close to his own thoughts and feelings and to make reflections on them. This is true for both older and younger children.

CHAPTER TWO

SOS!

Session one: 7 March

They say my son needs help

A t the appointed time, Fredrik comes running up all five flights of stairs, carrying his son. The receptionist has told him where he can hang up their outdoor clothes. However, they are still fully dressed, wearing their caps and gloves, when they arrive at our rooms. Fredrik just could not bring himself to sit in the waiting room. He preferred to wait on the sidewalk outside instead. They are all bundled up, because it is a cold day and they have walked a long way. We ask them to come into the playroom where Fredrik, Jorge and I sit down in the easy chairs. Victor has buried himself inside his father's jacket and is crying softly. He is distraught and wants to go home.

Fredrik is a nice-looking man in his thirties. He looks as if he would be the sporty type under normal circumstances. Now he has lost sleep and has dark rings under his eyes. His blond hair is tousled and from time to time he just stares into space. He tries to coax his son to come out from under his clothes, but Victor refuses to budge. Fredrik tries to take off his jacket and says, while holding

5

on to the boy, "Victor is never this shy. It's just that he feels weird in front of official people at official places."

Fredrik, who is already hard pressed by everything, is further stressed by the situation at hand and continues, "They say my son needs help. But I don't have the strength to face more authorities."

It seems as if neither father nor son knows exactly where they are, so Jorge tells Fredrik briefly about us and our work. Victor is still hidden under his father's jacket, but he has stopped crying. I presume that he is listening, so I say aloud, "Your dad has called us. He wants to get some help for the two of you. You're both very sad. We can help dads and little boys who are very sad. That's what we do here."

Victor does not stir, so we go on introducing ourselves. We also say that Jorge helps big people and I help little ones. I want to arouse his curiosity so I add, "We have things in this room that you can build with, if you want to. We have sand trays here. Next door is another room, where we can sit and talk if we want to. Today we're going to be together for quite a while, so there's no hurry. When we're finished, you and your dad are going back home together."

When Victor hears about going back home, he suddenly sticks out his swollen, tear-covered face and says, "St'oller too." I agree with him.

"Yes, it's important that you take the stroller home with you. That's how your dad gets you around. You mustn't forget the stroller. I'm glad you're thinking of that."

Victor is a pert little boy with blond hair and blue eyes. He is two and a half years old and is in nappies. He is not very tall for his age. After a short while, Victor's curiosity wins out over his crying and he lets his dad remove several layers of clothes.

After Fredrik has wiped his son's face and nose, Victor starts to look around. First he examines Jorge, who sits waiting cautiously next to his father. Then he looks at me for a long time and I nod reassuringly. Nobody speaks, and after a while I move over and sit down on the edge of the sand tray, saying, "Come here and take a look, if you want to."

Victor's dad takes him by the hand and they head straight for the shelf where all the toy cars are kept. Fredrik takes down several cars. Victor glances at each one and tells us its make. The private car is an Opel, the ambulance is a Mercedes, and so is the fire engine. The truck is a Volkswagen. They go through all the cars on the shelf except the black hearse. They do not touch that one. Now Victor also tells us which makes of cars various men in their circle of acquaintances drive. Dad nods approvingly. They also inspect the aeroplanes, boats, and trains, and then all the animals.

Dad goes back to Jorge, sits down and starts to talk with him. Victor notices the sand tray and wants to build in it. He gives me a questioning look and I tell him that he can use whatever toys he wishes. Immediately delighted, he looks at them and places some in the sand. He grabs all the horses he sees, both big and little ones, and places them upside down in the sand so that only their legs are showing. By not letting the horses stand right side up, he shows me how life appears to him. His entire existence has suddenly been turned upside down, just like the horses. He wants his father to look at the horses, but Fredrik cannot concentrate on them so Victor continues his play. He now seems unconcerned about why the two of them have come to us.

After a while Fredrik looks pleadingly at Jorge and we understand that he is eager for the two of them to speak in private. So I

Figure 1.   One of the first things Victor does is to put all the horses on their heads in the sand.
Comment. By not letting the animals stand on their feet, Victor shows how life looks to him. His life has suddenly been turned upside down.

suggest, "Come and let's go see the other room. It's nice for you to know what it looks like, too."

Once inside the room, Fredrik and Jorge sit down in the easy chairs. Victor hops about and looks around curiously, but soon concludes, "Other room more fun."

I ask him, "Do you want to go back to the other room with me? You can come to daddy any time, because the doors are open."

Victor hesitates a little, but wants to go back to the sand tray and the toys. He gives me his little hand, I take it, and we return to the playroom. I sit down next to the shelf with all the little dolls on it, to see if I can get him to join me there. He comes and picks out some dolls that represent male figures. He looks at them carefully, laughs out loud, and runs to show his dad an elderly man doll with very little hair. Fredrik looks at it and says that it resembles Victor's maternal grandfather. Victor gets a tired pat on his head from his father and runs quickly back to the sand tray in the playroom. He tries to find more dolls that represent men. He does not seem to see the others. I take a lady doll and hold it in my hand. I am looking at it without saying anything, unsure of whether Victor is paying any attention to it, when he suddenly says, "Only guys."

We talk about the doll that looks like his grandfather and I ask him, "What's your grandpa's name?"

Victor knows exactly what his first name is and says, "Grandpa name's Bertil, don't you know?"

He examines the animals, both wild and tame ones, and puts some of them in the sand. He wants me to help him secure the elderly men dolls on the back of the pig. Victor shows me precisely what he wants and I follow his directions. Three men are to sit on the back of the pig because they are going for a ride. He laughs excitedly as he gallops away with the pig, making all three dolls fall off.

I place a female doll in a nurse's uniform next to me and I wait for Victor to notice it. He looks cautiously at the doll and takes her up in his hand. He inspects her from the front and from the back for a long time as if this is an object that he does not recognize at all. As he is fingering the doll he sighs very deeply. After a moment I respond to his sigh and draw a sigh myself. By responding thus, I want to show Victor that in this place sorrow may be expressed in any way whatsoever. To sigh can be such an expression. We do not speak, but Victor sighs once more and I do as well. He continues his game with the elderly men dolls and the pig. After a while I return his attention to his own grandfather and ask, "So your grandpa's name is Bertil. And what's your grandma's name?"

Victor replies quickly, "I not know, never!"

The worst thing imaginable

Victor wants to stop playing and go to his dad. He does not want to think about grandmas or any other females, either in his imagination or in reality. When we enter the other room, he first takes a close look at his father's face and then climbs up into his lap. Fredrik puts his arms around Victor and gets a big hug in return. Fredrik looks somewhat less distressed than when he arrived.

We take up the question of whether they want to come back to see us and Fredrik answers, "I want to do everything possible for my son. He's all I have left. I want him to get all the help that's available but I just can't understand how you can help such a little child, who doesn't understand what has happened."

Fredrik cannot grasp how his son can be so upbeat when all the adults around him are devastated by grief. He is also concerned about the damage that might be done if the truth were to dawn on Victor too abruptly.

"Only someone who's really an expert on little children can get it across to them, in the right way, that something like this has happened," Fredrik says in a questioning voice.

We understand that he is concerned about our skills and experience, so we assure him that we are the experts he is talking about. We tell him that we see many children and parents who are undergoing severe difficulties in their lives. I ask him, "Is there anything that especially worries you about what might happen if Victor comes to see me?"

"Yes, that he'll cry and cry and die of grief when he understands what's happened to him and sees that both his and my life, our entire lives, have been destroyed. Then I have no one left."

We listen to Fredrik's fears and anxieties. He lets us know that he has come to us primarily on the urging of his mother and mother-in-law, as well as the day-care personnel. He says, "Honestly, I've never been to any place with a name that starts with psych. I'm not used to such things."

We discuss his fears and in the end I suggest that they return for two more visits during that same week. I need to meet Victor a couple of times to conduct a psychological assessment. After that, no doubt I can understand more about his way of reacting. By observing Victor's behaviour after the visits, Fredrik can see for himself how his son feels about coming to see me.

"Children usually want to come here," I assure him.

As we conclude the session, all of us return to the playroom. There we agree on the time for the coming two sessions. Fredrik takes out his pocket computer and enters the dates and times while I note them in my appointment book. When he has put away his computer, he says, "Yes, I think we'll be coming back. Everyone tells me Victor needs help, so why not give it a try?"

While Jorge confirms the time with Fredrik, Victor looks at the pen in my hand and asks, "What you write on your book?"

"I write that you will be coming back to see me in two days."

I understand from his curious glance that he wants to look in my appointment book. I therefore hasten to draw a little boy on the line for three o'clock, 9 March. Victor grabs my hand and pulls it toward him so that he can look in the book. He studies the boy I have sketched, looks me straight in the eye and says sternly, "Write my daddy there too!"

Deeply moved by Victor's concern for his father, I sneak a look at Fredrik out of the corner of my eye. He is completely absorbed by his own thoughts and does not notice. I squat down so that Victor is able to see the page in my book. I draw a dad holding his boy by the hand on the same dotted line. Fredrik then starts to dress the two of them in all their winter clothing. When they are ready, I tap Fredrik on the shoulder and tell them both to look at the figures I have drawn. At the same time, I "read" aloud from my appointment book, "Now it says here that Victor and daddy are coming back to see us on the ninth of March at three o'clock. That's in two days. It's decided. We'll be waiting for you then! It won't be long."

When they have gathered all their things together, Fredrik takes my hand and says, "We'll be seeing you."

"Yes. Good-bye till then."

Dad carries his son down the steps and Victor laughs and waves to us with his feet. He has his boots on the wrong feet, but nobody mentions it. Victor does not care. Fredrik does not notice it and we find it totally unimportant under these circumstances. It shows how their total existence is. Right or left does not matter at all.

While alone with Jorge, Fredrik has had time to tell about the situation he and his son are in. He needs to talk about the traffic accident, indeed about everything, but does not want to do so in Victor's presence. The catastrophe occurred two and a half months ago. The family had been on their way to celebrate Christmas with good friends. It was to have been little Oliver's first Christmas. All of a sudden they ran into black ice and a head-on collision could not be avoided. Fredrik's wife Malin and Oliver, who was six months old, died of internal injuries.

"I just can't grasp that they're gone. This is the worst thing that could happen to us, the worst thing imaginable," Fredrik tells Jorge.

Fredrik broke several ribs and suffered a concussion and cuts, but most of his injuries have healed by now. Victor was miraculously unhurt. Fredrik also tells Jorge about all the sorrowful and demanding things he has had to deal with since the deaths. At last these things are winding down. As he speaks he puts his arms around his head several times, as if to hold his thoughts together.

Fredrik does not remember much from the funeral. He walked around in a stupor with Victor at his side. Fredrik says it was lucky that he had Victor there, because he does not think he could have endured it otherwise. He tells Jorge that he feels totally alone in spite of his helpful family and friends. Even though Victor is so little, Fredrik finds him to be of great support, "strange as it may seem".

In answer to Jorge's question about how they managed the walk to our institute, he explains, "Actually, I tried it out yesterday evening. I came here with my mother-in-law and Victor, who was asleep in the stroller."

They had read the name of the Erica Foundation on the nameplate on the door and seen a light in a window. The building made a good impression on Fredrik's mother-in-law. It felt reassuring to know in advance how to reach their destination for the next day. They have been trying to help each other in general, Fredrik and his mother-in-law, but they are finding it hard, if not impossible. How can they support each other when they are both at a total loss, when they both need all their strength just to hold themselves together? Neither of them can sleep at night. They lie awake, turning things over and over in their minds. From this first meeting it seems clear to us that Fredrik needs help so that he in turn can help his son.

After father and son have left, Jorge and I need to rest a while to regain our own psychic balance. We remain seated for a long time after the workday is over, talking to each other. We are both deeply touched by the meeting with Victor and his father. A great tragedy has hit them and we have taken in their strong feelings of unreality and desperation. We both have a strong desire to deny that this has happened, at the same time as we know it has.

I tell Jorge that I read a notice in the paper about this traffic accident the day after it happened. It said that a two-year-old boy, incredibly enough, had escaped unscathed. Being a child psychologist, I always hope that children who survive such catastrophes will get the psychological help they need. So were my thoughts about this unknown two-year-old boy as well. Jorge and I both feel strong empathy for this young father, his son, and their relatives. Everything feels so unreal, so gripping, and so very, very sad.

Psychological assessment

Victor goes through a psychological assessment during the following two sessions. Fredrik wants to know what his son actually understands. I am trying to grasp what Victor has absorbed of the tragic event that has taken place. Does Victor know what happened? If so, what does he know, and in what way does he know it?

How has this severe trauma affected him psychically and socially? He has been through so much that can be traumatizing in the extreme. The death of his mother and baby brother, of course, the frightful experience of the accident itself, the changed behaviour of his father and all those surrounding him, plus being a survivor. Which one or combination of these is at the root of Victor's brave and cheerful outward behaviour?

For the psychological assessment, Victor will be spending time playing and interacting with me in the playroom. I will observe his behaviour and see what he is aware of as well as what he does not seem to be aware of. I will try to draw conclusions about how he really feels deep down inside, based upon what I see of his outward behaviour. Such an assessment cannot be expected to give the whole truth, but it should contribute to a deeper understanding of Victor's way of reacting.

A child's mourning reactions are determined to a large degree by his experiences in life before his loss. Fredrik's description of Victor's life before and after the accident is therefore an important part of the assessment and must be included in the final interpretation of the results. In addition to the conclusions I will draw from my observations, another aim of the assessment is to give Fredrik an opportunity to see how Victor and he himself feel about their visits with us. After all, the idea of seeking psychological help was not his own originally.

Fredrik needs some time to get used to the idea of coming to a psychiatric clinic. He is not negative towards our help, but he wonders intently how it can be possible to help a child of just two years of age. Despite his doubts, Fredrik repeats that he wants Victor to have the best possible help, if in fact he really needs any. He also wants to be assured that his son will not be put through something that will burden him even more.

The day after their visit, I get a call from Fredrik. He wants to reassure us that they will be back as planned. He has spoken with his wife's sister, his own parents and his parents-in-law. They all want Victor to go through the assessment and he himself has actually asked when he can come back and play in the sand tray again. I repeat the time for the two sessions we have planned during the present week. I also explain carefully that Jorge will not be present at the second session of the two. It will then be Fredrik, Victor and I who meet together. Unsure of whether Fredrik is registering the last point, I repeat it once more.

Fredrik does not want to hang up. He tells me that his father asked Victor what he did during his visit to us. Victor was quick to make up the answer that he had read books. Fredrik tells me he has noticed that Victor nowadays often makes up answers that will please the questioner. He knows that his grandfather likes to read books.

Fredrik takes a deep breath and says, "Do you think you can find out whether Victor understands that his mother and Oliver are dead and will never come back? What if he's expecting them to come back home?"

"I think I'll be able to understand much better how he feels inside and how he perceives his present life after the assessment," I answer.

He continues, "All his grandparents want to know what's really going on in Victor's mind. He just seems to get happier and happier and they worry that this isn't normal. They also wonder if he can already have forgotten his mother and Oliver. Can that really be possible?"

I assure him that I will do everything I can to answer his questions after the assessment. At that time I will tell Fredrik what conclusions I have reached and we will discuss possible treatment.

From my first encounter with Victor, I do wonder what he is denying most intensely. Is it the reality of the disappearance of his mother and Oliver or is it the overwhelming and impossible-to-handle feelings that come from inside himself? Which threats are the most painful, the inner or the outer ones, or both?

For the assessment we will use the two rooms where we first met. The room with the set-up for adult talks is referred to as Jorge's room, and mine as the playroom. The materials in the playroom remain the same: toys, dolls, paper and crayons. There were no books in the room before and there will not be any now, except for my appointment book. When Victor told his grandfather that he had read books, he may have had that book in mind. It is also possible that he referred to a book for children about death. His grandfather tried to read such a book for Victor, but he did not want to listen.

During the assessment I will focus solely on Victor's unique feelings and experiences and not bring up those of other children. Thus, I do not use any books that generalize and tell about others who have suffered a loss. Children who come to a psychological assessment always appreciate that the focus is entirely on their own individual self.

CHAPTER THREE

Session two: 9 March

Must I go on living?

Again Fredrik comes bounding up the stairs with his son on his arm. Before they reach the last steps, Victor leans out of his father's grip. He smiles and waves "happily" with his small hands, first to Jorge, then to me. All four of us go into the playroom and Fredrik starts to take off Victor's outdoor clothes. He is wearing brand new clothes today. When Fredrik has finished, Victor stands there in the middle of the room observing him.

When he sees that Fredrik shows no sign of either sitting down or taking off his coat, Victor moves closer to him. He is endearingly eager to make sure his father is doing all right. He motions to show Fredrik that he should remove his coat. He pulls at his jacket and grabs the lowest button, which is the only one he can reach. Fredrik removes his coat, but Victor wants him to take off his suit jacket as well, and he obeys. I take all their clothing and put it on the unoccupied easy chair. Fredrik takes out his mobile phone and turns it off. Victor notices this and seems pleased.

Fredrik and Jorge sit down in their easy chairs and start to talk while Victor and I go towards the toy cupboard. Victor is wound up and seems to like seeing the room and the sand tray again. He looks like a miniature man in his new clothes, bought for him to grow into. His new outfit is brown and includes jeans with a belt that fits in place above his nappy, a polo shirt with a sports insignia, a bandanna and shoes that look like real soccer shoes. I think to myself that these clothes were bought by a man, not a mother.

Victor is full of energy and studies the toys on the shelves that he is tall enough to reach. He wants me to share his joy of discovery and calls out cheerfully, "Oh, this is good! Look here! And look at this! Wow! Cool!"

He wants to show off what he knows and what he can do. I look at everything he does and all he shows me. He hops about, stamps on the floor, sits down on his nappied bottom and waves with a little toy cannon. Jorge observes Victor's clowning around as well, when there is a pause in his talk with Fredrik. Every time Jorge looks at him, Victor returns the glance with a searching expression in his eyes. Suddenly, everybody in the room hears Fredrik ask solemnly, "Must I go on living?"

Both Jorge and I turn towards him immediately and answer in unison, loudly and clearly, "Yes, you must, you absolutely must."

We are filled with empathy for Fredrik, whose life has become so hard. Victor stares at me and I nod my head affirmingly. He is suffering with his dad. This is obvious. The atmosphere in the room weighs down on us and it is difficult to find some words of true comfort. Even so, we do our best to remind them that there is help for their pain. I add, "The two of you have come to us for help now. We can help both children and dads."

Father and son look at each other. No one speaks. The silence is total. Victor goes over to Fredrik and climbs up in his lap. Fredrik gives him a sorrowful pat on the head. They sit this way for a while, until Victor's curiosity takes over. He wants to return to his play in the sand. He strokes his dad's cheek, laughs, and says that it feels prickly. Fredrik has not shaved for a couple of days. Victor slips out of his father's lap and runs over to the sand tray, where I am sitting. At Jorge's initiative, he and Fredrik go into Jorge's room to continue their conversation where they left off. I suggest to Victor that he stays with me. He does not object and starts to scoop up and pour out sand with a shovel.

Victor is an alert boy who is eager to learn. He wants to know about the toys he has never seen before. He asks me about the crocodiles, cannons, traffic signs, sailing ships, and polar bears. Then he runs around in the room till his blond hair is wet with perspiration. He searches the cupboard for as many dolls as possible that represent men. He finds some: an ordinary man, a king, a prince, a boy troll, a big boy and a small one. He also takes a careful look at the doctor, the stationmaster, the bridegroom, and the policeman. His favourites of all are the two dolls that are made to look like older men. One of them is grey-haired, and the other is the bald doll that he became fond of during his first visit. He gives me a questioning look. I nod and say, "You can use all the toys and dolls and do what you like with them. If you want to, you can make something with them in the sand tray."

Victor picks out some dolls and says, "Grandpas want ride. A daddy also ride. But him ride on somepin alone. Another man also there. Help to me!"

"Yes, I'll help you. Can you tell me how you want things to be?"

Victor tells me, "Put mens on an'mals. Make mens stick, have to make them stick."

He does not want them to fall off like they did last time, when they galloped around in the sand. The two older men are riding on an elephant, the daddy on a tiger, and the stationmaster on a pig. I fasten the men securely on the animals' backs. I help him with exactly what he wants, nothing else. He alone determines the pace and the direction of the game.

"All the mens look for their grandma," Victor tells me.

He searches everywhere in the room, under the sand tray frame and in the toy cupboard, but not on the shelf, where the grandma doll is lying in plain sight.

At one point Victor wants us both to crawl under the sand tray to look for grandma. I tell him that I am ready to help him look for her but I do not say that I will get down and crawl. We ride away with the animals and the dolls to the corner of the tray that he chooses, making the sand fly up as we go. He does not want the toys to get lost, so I keep watch over them as I squat there, next to the sand tray, ready to be of help. Victor takes a firm grip on one of my legs while he lies down flat on the floor to look for grandma under the sand tray. It seems to worry and frighten him a bit when

Figure 2. Two granddads, a dad and another man ride away to look for grandma, who has disappeared. They look all over the place but cannot find her.
Comment. Searching for something without finding it becomes an important theme in the process of working through grief.

he calls and calls under there but does not get any answer. He sighs, "Oh no, oh no. Thought so. Grandma gone."

"Yes, where can she be?" I ask.

"Prob'ly buying somepin to eat."

Suddenly, we hear some commotion from the stairway, and thereafter screams from an older child. Victor immediately calls for Fredrik, "What you doing, daddy?"

The doors are open between the two rooms, so his voice carries into Jorge's room. Jorge is the one who answers, "Dad and I are sitting here talking."

Victor runs to Fredrik and looks at him intently for a moment. When he is convinced that his dad is all right, he comes back to me and says, "What his name?"

He poses the question as he points to the chair in the playroom, where Jorge was sitting earlier. When I tell him Jorge's name, he recognizes it at once. He repeats it after me several times. It sounds like he is trying hard to pronounce it correctly in Spanish, as if it might stick in his mind better this way:

"Jorge, Jorge, Jorge."

I add, "Jorge is helping daddy."

Victor seems to collapse to the floor and starts flapping about down there. In a surprised and shrill voice he asks, "What help dad needs?"

He shivers, showing simultaneously his curiosity about, and his guard against, getting an answer to the question he has posed, so I simply reply, "Because dad is sad."

I understand that I must proceed very carefully and not say any more. Victor returns to his gleeful shouts and calls for me to look at all kinds of things that he fetches and throws in the air. I join him by looking at everything he wants me to look at, while at the same time observing everything that is going on. Among the toys are pieces of brown fencing and he wonders, "What's this?"

I do not want to steer the way he sees the toys and how they are to be used, so I say, "You can use them for whatever you wish."

He puts a few fence parts out in the sand and tells me that they are frying pans. He puts a little doll stove next to them. That the frying pans are many times the size of the stove does not bother a two-year-old. Victor becomes totally delighted with his creation. When he finds a cosy little white house with a red roof, he puts that alongside the stove. He shouts, clapping his hands, "I need that. I need all those things."

I agree. "Yes, you need good food to make you grow and a warm house so you don't get cold."

In Victor's precarious situation I can only reinforce his need for nurture and warmth, both physical and psychical. He is very persistent in his play, and adds a forest with many trees. It takes him much effort to get them to stand up in the sand. In the end he can hardly see the stove, the house, and the frying pans for all the trees that block the view. It looks as if everything becomes too painful when Victor's own needs come into focus. The game becomes calmer when he can no longer see the toys associated with his needs.

When the game is finished, Victor begins to rattle off all the colours he knows, and talks about storybook figures he likes. He can name many, and wants me to applaud his knowledge. He romps around, jumping on the floor so that his nappy bobs up and down. He wants to do whatever he can to create a sunny atmosphere in the room. He tries to get me to laugh and jump up and down as well. I motion to him that I do not want to jump and cannot laugh.

Instead I meet him half way by showing that I want to be together with him and that I respect all his attempts to master his sadness. I want to assure him that it is all right to babble, be noisy, and jump around, but, by remaining serious myself, I also want to convey to him that there are other ways to deal with grief.

Victor makes such a heart-rending impression, so capable and clever, speaking so clearly and knowing so many words. There he is, small enough for me to scoop up in the breadth of my hand, yet he is fighting so fiercely for his own and his father's survival. As I sit and watch him and his play, I experience a strong sense of unreality. At times I feel that the awful thing that has happened has not really happened after all, but is just some freak misunderstanding. I assume that this is how Victor feels inside himself and the only way he can "tell" me this is to make me feel the very same feelings.

When the session is over, we go and get Fredrik to come back to the playroom. Victor takes his father by the hand and shows him what he has created in the sand. Fredrik looks at the trees and the brown fences. He nods approvingly, but does not quite know what he is supposed to see in them. The process of getting dressed to go home begins. They have come warmly dressed and it takes quite a while to put on all their outdoor clothes. We remind Fredrik and Victor that Jorge will be out of town when they have their next appointment so the three of us will meet without him, as we have agreed. Fredrik has already been given this information, but he and Victor still look surprised. They do not want any changes.

Life before and after

While Victor and I are in the playroom, Fredrik tells Jorge about his desolation and about how he views their situation. The accident occurred two and a half months ago. An oncoming car slid over into their lane because of black ice and it was impossible for Fredrik to swerve aside. It was all over in a split second. Fredrik's wife Malin was in the front passenger seat and little Oliver was strapped into a baby car seat on the seat behind her. It was their side of the car that was hit by the sliding car. Fredrik was cleared of any responsibility for what happened, but he has a strong sense of guilt nevertheless.

Since the day of the accident Victor has not asked for his mother or for his little brother. A call for his mum has not slipped out of his mouth one single time, despite his previous habit of calling to her quite often. Only once, when Victor called for his dad and Fredrik responded, did it seem clear that Victor had hoped for his mother to appear. For a second he looked disappointed, but then quickly changed his expression.

Fredrik says that he finds it remarkable that Victor does not ask about his mother's whereabouts. His wife, a colourful person who took centre stage in the family, had been at home full-time with the children. Victor's light blue "blankie" disappeared that day, and he has never once asked for that either. He could never fall asleep without it. They brought him home from the maternity ward wrapped in that blanket and it had always been with him.

Fredrik continues to recount his feelings, "I panic at the very thought that I won't be able to cope with everything alone. Some days it feels like my head's going to burst from all these thoughts."

Jorge wants to know, "What's the very worst of all?"

"Everything's the worst, everything's just as horrible!"

His body aches all over. He knew that pain from broken ribs could last a long time but he has been told that those injuries have healed. The pain from his ribs was nothing compared to the pain he has now. Fredrik has had several medical examinations but the doctors have not been able to identify the cause of his pain. He says, "Maybe my pain is caused by my emotional state, some kind of psychological thing. I'm starting to believe so myself."

Jorge tells him that he is probably right. Fredrik continues, "I feel like I've been beaten black and blue. I forget things, can't concentrate, can't make head or tail of anything. I don't know whether I'm coming or going. Nothing matters any more."

Fredrik talks about how he met Malin eight years ago at the university where they were both studying. She took a degree in journalism and was working for one of the daily newspapers. At the time of the accident she had been taking leave to be at home with the children. Fredrik is a civil engineer and is working as head of security at a computer company. It is clearly a demanding job with a high level of responsibility. He appreciates his colleagues, who are showing great compassion now and giving him the freedom to come and go as he is able.

Fredrik tells Jorge today, as during the first visit, that he has had to attend to many wrenching tasks related to the deaths of his wife and son. He can no longer stand to see the envelopes that typically come from the authorities when a family member passes away. His father now opens his mail and decides whether it needs Fredrik's attention or not.

Fredrik and Victor live in a suburb of Stockholm, in the terraced house to which they moved last year right before Oliver's birth. Now Fredrik finds it very hard being in the house. It feels much too big and lonely. Malin and he had purposely waited to have children till they were both established in their careers. Yet they were the first among their siblings and friends to have children. Victor goes to a day-care centre and he loves being there. His favourite teacher's name is Lotta. Fredrik urges Jorge to have me talk to her about how everything is going for Victor at the centre. The staff there want him to have psychological help, because they can see that he needs help beyond what they can give.

Fredrik and Victor have many relatives who want to be of help. Both Fredrik's parents, Grandpa Erik and Grandma Maria, are pensioners. His two younger brothers, Johan and Anton, are identical twins, twenty-two years of age. They live at home with their parents in a neighbouring suburb. The in-laws, Grandpa Bertil and Grandma Marianne, live in the same suburb as Fredrik. He explains that he and Malin had bought the house there in order to be close to them. Malin's sister, Anna, has her own family, a husband and a one-year-old daughter. The entire family, except Malin's brother Martin, who is studying abroad, live around Stockholm. There are no long distances between them.

Fredrik describes his son as a happy and curious boy. Victor has never used much baby talk. When he started to speak it was with clear diction from the start. He is outgoing, chatty and easy to love, wherever he is. Malin's mother maintains that he takes after Malin in this regard. Victor keeps a check on all his relatives, knows their names and loves to talk to them on the phone. When Fredrik talks about his son his eyes light up and he exudes obvious warmth.

Many people have trouble telling Fredrik's twin brothers apart, since they look and act very much alike. Victor, however, has always known who is who, even on the telephone. This is in spite of the fact that their voices are so much alike that Fredrik always has to ask with whom he is speaking. Victor likes Anton best. Anton was the one who noticed that Victor needed new clothes and bought things that would "look good on a young lad".

Since the accident Victor has become "precocious, generous, and helpful". He eats well, likes all foods and sleeps well, never waking Fredrik at night. This used to happen frequently in the past. Before the accident Victor had started potty training. Now the potty has somehow disappeared and the training has been put off for the time being.

Almost everything to do with Victor is actually working well, as long as nobody mentions anything about his mother or Oliver. A mere word, a photo, or the mention of the cemetery disturbs his inner balance. Victor then responds by playing the clown, showing off his abilities, chattering loudly or singing. Whenever he sees someone crying, he will go to any lengths to make that person happy again. Such persevering and touching efforts always end up making people cry even more. The adults feel that they ought to be the ones consoling Victor, instead of the reverse. However, it does not always work this way.

Jorge and I both experience strong feelings of unreality and we both have splitting headaches after today's session. We are saddened and deeply moved after our meeting with Victor and his young dad. Both of us gratefully acknowledge the value of working together so that we can share our experiences and support each other. What we are encountering is tragic beyond words.

CHAPTER FOUR

Session three: 13 March

Hold my daddy's hand!

Today, both Fredrik and Victor look a bit more at peace when I see them coming up the stairs. Victor wants to climb the last flight of stairs, a narrow one, by himself. Fredrik puts him down and he starts to climb, as little children do, one step at a time. He plants both feet on each stair step and holds on with both hands to the step above. It takes some time, but Victor manages. He looks around hesitatingly as he enters the playroom and asks immediately for Jorge. I remind him that Jorge is not going to be here today, as we told him earlier. Father and son also discussed this matter before they came today. Victor is obviously concerned about Jorge's absence and remains standing in the hallway.

I ask them to come into the playroom, because Victor is standing dangerously close to the stairway. His dad helps him take off his outdoor clothes and boots. However, Victor is much more interested in helping Fredrik to get out of his clothes. He reaches up on his tiptoes and pulls at Fredrik's coat, his scarf, and his gloves. When they are all off, Victor drags his own and his father's clothes to the chair where I put them last time. He wants things to be like they were earlier. After pushing all the clothing together in a pile on the chair, he pats his dad's clothes and says softly, "It's okay. It's okay."

Victor sounds as if he is trying to console his father's coat. Fredrik excuses himself and says he needs to go to the restroom. I can see that he wants to give Victor the opportunity to be alone with me in the playroom. I tell Fredrik that he can sit where he wants to, in the other room, in the playroom or in the hall. When he returns from the restroom, he pokes his head into the playroom and says that he will sit and wait on a chair in the hall. As Fredrik closes the door, Victor is already engrossed in inspecting the toys he has not yet had time to see.

Victor has looked forward to coming back. After two sessions he feels at home with the sand trays, the toys, Jorge and me. He has decided who belongs to which easy chair in the room. He wants his surroundings to be as they were on their first visit. He points to the chair that belongs to Jorge and to the one he wants me to sit in. He intends to share Fredrik's chair, since he sat on his dad's lap during the first session. One chair is thus left over, and that one is to be for the clothing, exactly as it is arranged today. It is important for Victor that order is maintained. He goes to the chair that belongs to him and his dad. He sits up in it and, leaving plenty of room beside him, he says, "This daddy place."

"Yes, next to dad you have a good spot," I answer.

He is keen to fantasize that Fredrik is actually sitting next to him now. He says, "He sit here. He really is."

"Yes, you want to be next to dad. He wants to be next to you, too. You think about him a lot. Daddy's waiting for you."

Victor is still wondering about Jorge:

"Where is he? What he doing? When he back?"

Victor does not like empty chairs. He is upset about the fact that Jorge is not in his chair talking with his father, but is somewhere else. I tell him, truthfully, "Jorge will be back tomorrow."

Victor responds instantly, "Daddy come back then."

"Yes, you want daddy to see Jorge and talk to him. Is that so?"

Victor nods his head and stands up in order to walk over to me. He suddenly stumbles and I seize his hand to prevent him from falling. He regains his balance, but keeps a firm grip on my thumb. He is still thinking of his dad and Jorge and wonders, "What they do?"

"They talk to each other."

"They hold hands, too?"

I answer simply, "Yes. Daddy feels better then."

Victor starts to chant to himself, "Hold my daddy's hand! Hold my daddy's hand!"

Fredrik has overheard our talk from where he is sitting outside the room. He has been trying to concentrate on his newspaper, but has to clear his throat and reach for his handkerchief. He is moved by his son's concern for him.

Victor bounds over to the toy cupboard. He wants to look at the toys on the second shelf, but he is too small to reach them. He drags over a small chair, props it on the sand tray and starts to climb. I get up close to be ready to lend him a hand. It looks somewhat unsteady, but he manages to get up on the chair. He laughs and jokes about the things he finds up there, giving them imaginary names. I hold on to the chair. He thinks that I cannot see the toys on the shelf when I stand on the floor, just as he could not see them a moment ago.

After a while he gets a glimpse of the things even higher up, on the third shelf. He asks me to take down the toys he points to. I lift him up instead, and let him pick whatever he wants. I am struck by how small and light his body is. At last the floor is full of toys that he has taken down. I suggest that he can play in the sand with some of them now, if he wants to. He answers me with a tone of authority, "Gotta clean up first."

In his voice I can hear his day-care teachers' words. He starts cleaning up by moving things around and rearranging them as well as he can. Most toys are moved to different parts of the room. I offer to help to re-establish the order that he needs so very much and I do what he tells me to do.

Only guys

Victor starts to look for toys to play with in the sand tray. He has a good memory. He remembers exactly the colours of all the different trains, cars, and aeroplanes, as well as the makes of the cars. He drives the cars around in the sand for a while, but stops and does not want to continue. Instead, he searches for the animals he played with during the previous session, the pig, the tiger, and the elephant. His search takes a long time and absorbs him completely. He giggles and plays the clown when he finds the animals and exchanges the pig for a bull. He tries to find the men dolls. They also have to be the same ones as last time, even though there are many others to choose from. He looks and looks for the grandfather dolls. He shows clearly that he does not want any more changes in his life.

"Gotta be here," Victor complains.

He does not find them, even though they are lying there in plain sight on a shelf next to the one where he found them last time. While he is searching, he mumbles quietly, "Messed up, messed up."

It disturbs him that other children have moved the toys about since he was here last. They are not in exactly the same place. I have anticipated that this could be disturbing for Victor and made a concerted effort to restore the order known to him in the room. Obviously, I have not been observant enough. At last he finds the dolls he is looking for. He smiles at me and states contentedly, "These the same. Gotta be two grandpas. It gotta be. I know."

On a tiger and a bull the grandfathers ride around and around in the sand tray. Sand swirls all over the room. Victor is laughing as he runs around the sand tray in order to make the animals gallop here and there. He stumbles several times in an unexpected manner. It looks as if he is about to lose his balance, but he does not. It looks strange, as if he is buckling under from a heavy burden. One or both of his knees give out for a second.

When Victor has calmed down a little, I say, "Now you're going to see some pictures. Look at them first and then you get to tell me what you see in them."

The test that he is going to do consists of pictures of animals and their young in different everyday situations. It is really meant for older children, who can be expected to create a little story about each picture. A two-year-old cannot do so, but he can perhaps say something about what is there in the pictures. I show Victor the first three pictures and everything goes smoothly. He sees and identifies baby birds eating porridge, bear cubs playing together, and a lion cub sitting in a chair. He refers to all the animals as baby animals. He does not observe that there are in fact animal mums and dads together with their young.

I hesitate for a while about whether to show him the fourth picture or not. Victor thinks I am too slow and snatches it from my hand. When he sees the picture he screws up his eyes and covers his ears. The picture shows a kangaroo mum with one of her young in her pouch and another, bigger one next to her. This is too much for Victor, as I sensed it would be, but too late. He runs out into the hall to his father, stands close to him, and holds on to his trouser leg for a while. I remain in the playroom and hear how they talk softly with each other.

After a while I go to the hall and say, "Yes, I know, you didn't like looking at that picture. Come back and we'll do something else."

He goes along with me to the playroom but he absolutely refuses to look at any more pictures, so I put them away. He shows clearly that he cannot stand to be reminded of mums and their babies. He wants instead to pull out all the cars, aeroplanes, dolls, trains, and lots of other toys. He wants all these toys to be in the chair that he considers as his and his father's.

"I do want to help you," I say.

He takes the toys off the shelves and puts them all in my lap. I bunch up my skirt around the toys and carry them to the chair. He unloads the toys and places them on both his own and his father's half of the chair. It is as if he wants to fill an empty space in himself as well as in his father with things that he likes, toys.

The chair is completely filled with toys. Victor heaves himself up and seats himself on top of the whole pile. He remains there as we make small talk and he looks as if he is sitting on a throne with his little legs dangling down. He hums a children's song, with his hands placed firmly around the arm rests, and he beams like a prince. The session is coming to an end and I suggest that we call on his dad to join us. Fredrik knocks first and then enters. He sits down in the empty chair that is meant for Jorge. Victor does not accept this and shouts, "No! Wrong! You sit your place."

Fredrik fetches their clothes and sits down on the outer edge of the chair filled with toys. It gets crowded in the chair, with Victor and Fredrik and all the toys. Victor does not want to go home today! Fredrik tries to get him interested by mentioning things that he knows his son likes, "Auntie Anna's coming today, so we must hurry home."

Victor looks straight at his father and asks seriously, "That really be any fun?"

His dad answers, taken aback, "You always enjoy seeing her."

That may well have been the case earlier, but Victor is obviously right in feeling that it is no fun to see his aunt now, after the accident. She cannot be happy. Nobody else they see can manage to be happy either.

Victor digs his fingers tensely into the chair arms. I tell him that next time his daddy will come alone to talk to me. We are going to talk about whether we can be of any more help to them. Fredrik looks surprised that I tell Victor this, so I explain, "Victor wonders what's going to happen. He wants very much for the two of you to come to us some more."

"Yes, I notice that," answers Fredrik.

He looks moved and glances at his son. Victor sighs deeply and so do I. Even though Victor is so reluctant to end this session, he slides down from the toy pile and starts the process of dressing for outdoors. When he is dressed and ready, Victor tries to get his dad to carry him down the steps upside-down. Fredrik declines and instead carries him off on his arm in the usual way. Victor whines softly, but halfway down he gives his dad a big bear hug.

Telephone conversation with Victor's favourite teacher.
16 March

A whole day-care centre rocked to its foundation

I make a phone call to Victor's day-care centre to hear how he is doing. I speak with his favourite teacher, Lotta. She is glad that Fredrik has sought help for Victor and explains that she and the staff have spoken to the father about the need for Victor to see a child psychologist. They are deeply concerned about him and do not know how to behave towards him. They are afraid of hurting him even more.

According to Lotta, Victor has not shown signs of sadness or cried after the accident. Surely there must be something strange about that? She describes Victor as a cheerful-natured and secure little boy, liked by both children and adults. He is curious and has well-developed speech. Before the accident Victor spent a set numbers of hours daily at the centre, but now they determine the length of stay with Fredrik day by day.

Lotta says that no one on the staff has ever before been through something as horrible as this. It has been and continues to be very difficult for them to cope. They have all been shocked, she says, and she is anxious to tell me how they first dealt with the tragic news about Victor's family. When Fredrik called Lotta a few days after the accident to tell her and the others about the death of his wife and baby, it took a long time for his words to sink in. Lotta simply could not comprehend what he was saying. She froze completely and told him that she would have to end the conversation. She would have to call him back.

As soon as she could gather the strength to do so, she called her two team-teachers and asked them to meet her at the centre. They were all shocked and deeply saddened, but they had to pull themselves together to plan how they would tell the other children and their parents. How do you confront children, between one and three years of age, with such horrible news? They spent a long time conferring and decided that they had to gather their courage, give each other support, and go to Victor and Fredrik's home together.

Victor was delighted that his teachers came to visit him. He behaved as usual and did not acknowledge that everyone around him was crying. Lotta wonders if this can be normal. Fredrik wanted Victor back at the centre as soon as possible. He also asked the teachers to tell the other children and parents about what had happened, preferably the next day. Victor's teachers contacted all the enrolled families that very evening. All the parents got together the following morning and most of them spent the day with their children at the centre.

The adults spoke with each other and with the children about what had happened to Victor's mother and baby brother Oliver. The whole centre seemed to be rocked to its foundation. One of the fathers, a fireman, who has seen many people in crisis, became and is still a pillar of strength. Lotta tells me how the teachers struggle with themselves in order to face each new day. One of her colleagues, whose mother died recently, has taken sick leave. She could not carry this added psychic burden.

Everyone was worried about how it would be for Victor to return to the centre. In fact it has transpired "all too easily". Lotta feels that it is unreal. There must be something that is locked up inside the boy. I ask her to give me examples of his actions, to help me understand better.

Lotta describes how all the children have their own albums with snapshots of their families. It happens from time to time that a child cries and longs for his mother. Victor then goes and fetches the child's album, and points to pictures of the child's mother. Consolingly, he reassures the child that his or her mother will be coming soon. When looking in his own album, he flips quickly by the pages with pictures of his mother and little brother. Instead he goes right to a picture of his twin uncles and explains laughingly who is who.

Recounting these aspects of Victor's situation over the telephone, Lotta starts to cry. She says it is almost too much to bear when Victor does things like this. I fully understand. I also find what she says intensely painful to listen to. Lotta concludes our conversation by expressing how much the staff appreciate that Victor is getting help now. It eases their burden to know that the responsibility for his well being is now being shared by a professional. As an aside, Lotta tells me that she has received her training as a day-care teacher relatively recently, and that she was not given so much as one hour's training in how to handle a crisis situation. From our conversation I understand how much help the staff have been to Victor and Fredrik, and I acknowledge this to Lotta.

CHAPTER FIVE

Results of assessment and choice of treatment

Session four: 21 March

A "happy" and capable boy in shock

As we have decided, Fredrik comes to see me alone to find out the results of the psychological assessment. We need to discuss Victor's psychic condition and Fredrik's thoughts on whether I can be of further help to his son. As soon as we are seated in our chairs in the playroom, Fredrik asks, "Can you tell me how Victor is doing? I mean, how he's really doing?"

"Victor has shown me a lot during the three sessions we have had. For one thing, he's really made it clear that he's eager to come here, both for his own sake and for yours," I answer.

I summarize my impressions of Victor for Fredrik. "Victor is a capable and harmonious boy to the core. He shows all the characteristics of a child who is surrounded by a loving family and given plenty of stimulation. He is sweet, full of initiative, curious, and easy to like. Victor speaks well and has learned many difficult words. Based on what I observe, I can guess that many people treat him as if he were an older child, even though he's in nappies and not especially tall for his age.

Fredrik nods and says, "I also tend to forget, sometimes, that he's only two years old."

Fredrik wants to hear more, so I continue, "He makes contact with me in a trusting way. He's quite open to playing and chatting during our sessions. He utilizes every moment he is here. He prefers that we have fun and wants to make me laugh. The atmosphere thus created in the room is a contradictory one, with a strong tension between joy and sorrow. It gives me a headache and I get a feeling that I'm going to be sick. This is the way Victor makes me understand how he feels inside."

Fredrik listens in amazement and asks me to explain what I mean.

"For a little child in this kind of extreme situation, emotional outlets like crying and moaning are not enough. Victor has 'deselected' them as expressions of his sorrow. When someone is too young to use the spoken language, he still has the language of emotion, which is a stronger language. Victor has sensed that I'm ready to contain what he has inside. He has therefore shown me this by making me feel the same feelings as he feels. So, you see, at times I've taken on his feelings."

I think to myself that Victor may not exactly have a headache, as I do, but he has trouble sorting out his thoughts, as when a person has a headache. What I associate with feeling sick shows up in Victor when his body seems to be out of balance. He is not stable and wobbles sometimes in a manner that has nothing to do with his young age. We reflect for a moment on what I have just said, and also talk about the strong feeling of unreality that Victor spreads around him. In my case this leads to my having to remind myself of why he is coming to see me.

Fredrik says that he has never thought about the situation in this way. He wants to hear more, so I go on.

"I see during the assessment that Victor's spontaneous joy has become exaggerated, exhilarated activity. He's in constant motion, is wound up, and sometimes flaps about like a clown. He senses an empty space within both himself and his dad and it frightens him, so he tries to fill it with hyperactivity, chatter, laughter, and lots of other things.

After a short pause I continue, "Victor also shows that he doesn't tolerate even the slightest change in his environment, which I think is entirely understandable. He's troubled by every little change in the room and considers everything destroyed when other kids have moved toys around on the shelves. Victor had a stable existence with predictable daily routines, and now everything has been changed in one fell swoop. Of course, every single person you two meet acts differently towards you than they did before. This means that everyone and everything are different in a way that Victor does not recognize, and it confuses him. Children have a particularly hard time with such changes."

I ask Fredrik what he thinks about my comments.

"I think all these changes are very hard, as well. Sometimes I just don't go to the shops, because I don't want to see others looking at me. What else have you found? I want to know everything that came out during the assessment," he says.

Fredrik is straining himself, trying to gather his thoughts. He says that he must really concentrate to keep his train of thought. I continue, "Nobody you two know is happy. Victor has seen it as his job to be happy for everyone else. If he succeeds in making a family member just a little bit happy, it reminds him of how it was earlier, when they weren't so unhappy and strange. If they laugh just a little, perhaps everything's back to normal after all and the awful thing never happened. In a two-year-old's magical way of thinking, everything then seems to be as it always has been, and so mother must be coming home soon.

Fredrik says sadly, "Poor Victor. It looks as if he's in the same muddle as me. I can also get such an overpowering feeling that they'll be coming back."

"So, you see, your relatives are right in their fear that Victor is waiting for his mother and Oliver to come back home. He hopes like everybody else. It's only natural to cling to hope under these circumstances," I say.

My experience tells me that it cannot be otherwise. Being two-and-a-half years old, Victor lives in the now, but is slowly starting to understand that there's something called yesterday and tomorrow. He obviously expects tomorrow to be a continuation of the day that is, which also should mirror the day that was. All days should thus resemble each other, to his way of thinking.

Time's context has been inexplicably broken for Victor. Right now, nobody in his immediate environment is able to instil any hope about the future. They have their hands full just coping from moment to moment. Victor is the one on whom Fredrik and all their relatives are concentrating, trying to understand and help. They hook their will to live on to him. For his sake they must all keep struggling. It can be a heavy burden for a little child to sense that those who are dear to him continue to exist only because he exists. Their well being is thus dependent on him.

Fredrik looks weighed down by his thoughts. We rest a while before I say, "Victor stumbles at times when he's moving around. It looks as if his knees are giving out."

"Yes, I know. I also see him doing that at home now. Neither his day-care teachers nor I saw anything like that earlier. It started after he came here," Fredrik adds.

"I think this is Victor's way of showing that he has trouble holding himself up. This refers to both body and soul," I explain.

Fredrik sighs heavily and asks, "Does Victor know that his mum and Oliver are gone forever?"

Victor no doubt answered this question best himself when he buried big and little horses halfway in the sand with their legs up in the air. He was also anxious to show Fredrik these scenes, so I say, "I think Victor both knows and doesn't know. He knows what a two-and-a-half-year-old is capable of knowing. Remember how he buried those horses? Well, horses that are buried with their heads in the sand and their legs in the air can't move. They can't do any of the things horses usually do, run, jump or live. I believe Victor wanted to show you that he knows, even if he doesn't comprehend the finality of death."

"Now when you mention what he did, well, I did not, could not, see that before on my own," says Fredrik.

"To see the legs sticking up out of the sand reminds Victor of the horses, even though they're buried. If you can see the hooves you know the horses are there, albeit under the sand. You don't forget them. They are there but at the same time they are not there, but perhaps they're somewhere anyway . . ."

Fredrik looks sorrowful and bewildered. After a pause I continue, "Children who have experienced the loss of someone dear to them use animals and dolls like this. They often symbolize their experiences through such play."

Fredrik wonders what thoughts Victor has about Oliver. It has been hard for me to get a grip on that and I tell him so. "It's not easy to differentiate Victor's mourning for his mother from that for his little brother. Oliver was close to his mother the whole time and the mourning for the two belongs together. He misses them together and this shows that he had incorporated Oliver into the family."

Fredrik tells me, "Victor never had any problems to speak of when it came to accepting Oliver's birth. Well, okay, one time he did ask his mother to send the baby back where it came from, but only once."

Fredrik has spoken to the teachers at the day-care centre and heard about what Victor does with the photo albums. We talk about how touched everyone is when Victor consoles others, both big and little ones, instead of asking for solace himself. Although he is the most needy one, he shoulders the role of the consoler. I say what I think. "It's probably less painful for him to be the one who gives rather than the one who needs consolation. If he were to receive consolation, he would be far too painfully reminded of why he needs it."

Victor consoles the other children at the centre when they want their mummies. He thereby denies that his own mother is also absent. After all, a child really misses his mother only if she is truly absent. If Victor denies intensely enough that she is gone, she will reside in his magical fantasy. Then he does not have to ask where she is. This is his way of trying to handle the horrifying thoughts that threaten him whenever his own mother is mentioned. He cannot localize the threats he feels, does not know if they come from inside or outside himself.

To a large degree Victor is also horrified to see his father so terror-stricken, a totally alien experience for him. Normally, his father is never afraid. To a certain degree the psychological assessment has contributed to making Victor's catastrophic reality start to move in on him. This is taking the form of a huge, emerging sense of loss towards those who have disappeared. The objects he has chosen and the games he has played during the sessions have started to open up his senses. It is thus becoming harder for him to continue denying the frightful truth.

Also, Victor has not shown any signs of missing his "blankie". At the age of two a blankie helps if you are a little sad or a little tired. However, it will not be of any help against overwhelming feelings such as those that threaten Victor, feelings he has never experienced before. Also, the security that the blanket used to give perhaps reminds him all too much of his mother. The blanket might have smelled like her or it might have given him a strong sense of calm connected to her. Either way, concretely or psychologically, the blanket can no longer be of help to him.

We continue speaking about the assessment. "Victor wants to do whatever it takes to avoid games that could conceivably include a mum. He guards against doing this forcefully no matter what material we use, dolls, animals, or pictures. If he cannot do anything to avoid it, he shuts off his sight and hearing by closing his eyes and putting his hands over his ears. By closing off his senses, he prevents any information that he cannot handle from reaching him. This way of protecting himself is very demanding for Victor. He must be on guard at all times and react quickly to anything and everything that could be threatening."

Finally, I want Fredrik to know that, even though I have come up with lots of observations, there are still questions I cannot answer.

"I get no leads into what he remembers from the accident itself. The loss of his mother and Oliver overshadows everything."

Fredrik repeats what he has already told us. "I don't know if Victor was asleep when it happened or if he fell asleep afterwards."

"Even if Victor was asleep at the moment of the violent collision, it must be assumed that what he experienced remains inside him in some form of body memory. You need to look out for signs of what he experienced and remember that these signs may not appear until later on."

Crisis therapy eases pain

It is now three months since the accident and the "happy" façade that Victor has been holding up is beginning to be too much of a strain on him. It cannot last any longer. Therefore it is not enough now for Victor to avoid mother figures. He avoids all female figures in his play. The way he has "chosen" will no longer lead him anywhere. A little boy cannot deny those on whom he depends.

Victor needs help directing the kind of feelings he has had for his mother to other women, and to men as well, for that matter. Victor wants to help his father in all possible and even impossible ways. After all, he is just over two years old. He demonstrates in his concrete and capable manner that he wants to get other grown-ups to help his father. Dad needs someone to hold his hand and Victor is resolute in his efforts to arrange this. When we talk about how Victor wants to help his dad, I can see from Fredrik's reactions that there are very deep and warm bonds between father and son.

On a psychological level, father and son have changed roles to some extent. Victor now gives his father the same care as he himself has received from his mother and father. Fredrik is greatly moved and again amazed that his son can show such things. I explain, "It's touching to see Victor's great concern about making a place for you on the chair, whether you're there in person or only in his imagination. He very precisely measures out two halves of the chair. He needs to feel your presence when his inner emptiness gets too frightening."

"You know, I don't see those things," says Fredrik.

"Well, actually, it often takes an outsider to notice. Victor shows these things more clearly when you're not with him. He pretends that you're sitting in the chair, when you're in fact in the other room talking to Jorge. Sometimes he looks in on you to make sure you're still there and that you're okay," I say, and continue, "Victor's play centres around the themes of disappearing, seeking and finding. This characterizes his whole world. Sometimes he can really find things that he wants us to look for, sometimes not. He doesn't always want us to find lost objects, even if they're right there before our eyes."

Fredrik is deeply moved about how much his son has been able to convey of his psychic condition through play during these sessions. Also, he thinks that Victor has been calmer after these three visits. He is moved by the strength of his little boy and says, "Last night was very difficult and I was even more desolate than usual. Then Victor said that we should go to 'the Erica' and started towards the door. I had to promise him that I would pull myself together. When he heard that word together, he understood me to say that we'd go to 'the Erica', both of us, together, and settled for that."

I go on, "Victor shows in both words and actions that he needs another form of help in addition to all the support he already gets. He shows a need for a space of his own, where he can express himself and his sorrow and receive psychic nourishment. He needs a place and a person that are not caught up in all the terrible things that have happened. His existence has been changed to the very core and this has become altogether too hard for him to master."

Victor has not wanted to tell one single person about what we have done during our sessions. Nor has Fredrik felt that he should ask. Integrity is important for both father and son.

"To be perfectly frank, Victor's response to these visits has taken me completely by surprise," says Fredrik.

"In what way do you mean?" I ask.

"It astounds me that he's understood what kind of place this is. How's that possible for a boy of only two and a half? Victor has grasped that faster than I have," says Fredrik.

I tell him that most children experience a psychological assessment as something new that they are taking part in. They appreciate the interest that the psychologist shows in them. They sense that they can get some type of help they need, even if they do not understand how this will happen. Most children appreciate, just like Victor, that their parents also are getting help from a grown-up. This unburdens them, so that they can concentrate on their own problems.

I describe crisis therapy for little children. "It's a psychological treatment method used to ease pain after a major trauma. The aim is to help the child live as full and harmonious a life as possible, in spite of the great loss. It's important for Victor to get a chance to work through his feelings and reactions, so that his development can continue. He has taken on certain strategies in order to survive, but some of these are not really working and he needs help to change them."

Fredrik listens and agrees that it is important to clear away all obstacles for Victor. I summarize and point out that he is a little over two years old and by all rights should be in the first stage of defiance. At this point children start to assert their own will, insist on doing everything themselves, and want to do it their own way. However, since the accident, Victor has become extremely docile and concerned with others' needs. He never insists on having his way and is exaggeratedly clever and funny. Such a gifted child should not have to develop into the class clown when he gets older, just because he does not dare to engage in a serious conversation. It is also risky in other ways to become too set on satisfying others' needs at the expense of his own. Victor must get help to return to the right track in his development. The psychological balance between father and son must also be reinstated.

"Do you think crisis therapy will help Victor?" Fredrik asks.

"I can give you an unequivocal yes in answer to that question. A treatment period of a couple of months will help you both. Victor is a secure boy, so he has good prospects for forming a trusting relationship with a therapist. This in turn provides a favourable basis for the working-through process."

I also tell Fredrik that I have the same opinion as Victor, that his father also needs more help, as a complement to the support he gets at the hospital. Jorge, who is not here today, has previously told Fredrik the same thing. During the course of our talk, Fredrik has started to look more and more relieved. He says, "You know, it's really mind-boggling to think that I have such a wise son."

I agree wholeheartedly. "Yes, he's very wise indeed, your little one."

Fredrik wants to know more about what crisis therapy will involve for his son, so I tell him. "Victor and I will work with the concrete issues that come up in his play. It's my responsibility to keep the focus on obstacles to Victor's grieving process. I'll also make sure that the pace of the treatment is the right one."

Fredrik has been afraid that Victor will be overwhelmed by his own feelings. He is so quick to throw himself into everything he does, but working through a trauma must not go too fast. In a little child the healing process can never be forced.

Fredrik tells me that the nurse whom he sees once a week has been most supportive. "She's helped me keep my head above water. She says that we can go on with our talks and I am really thankful for that. I talk to her mostly about myself and my own situation, not so much about Victor. She's told me that she has no experience with little children in grief."

Fredrik has thought of asking us for help for himself in order to better understand his son's reactions and how to respond to him. He points out, as he has before, the difficulty inherent in the fact that Victor is the oldest child in their family and immediate circle of friends. Thus, Fredrik has little experience of children Victor's age, only of younger ones.

We decide on time-limited crisis therapy for Victor with me, and supporting sessions for Fredrik with Jorge. The sessions will take place once a week for another two and a half months. I stress the need for continuity in the treatment, which means they must come every week. Fredrik has impressed us as being able to commit to such a schedule, both psychologically and practically. Even though they have to walk a long way to get here and it takes considerable psychic energy to begin therapy, Fredrik is strongly motivated about getting help for Victor.

A condition for Victor's therapy is that Fredrik accompanies him every time. The son must be assured that his father is also getting help. Only then can he begin to acknowledge his own needs and deal with his own grief. In order to get as full a picture as possible of the therapy process, I will also need to know what is happening to Victor in his everyday life. Such information will come out in Fredrik's talks with Jorge, who can pass it on to me.

Jorge and I will talk to each other after every session, which gives me a chance to keep Jorge up to date on how the healing process is going for Victor. Jorge will then share this information with Fredrik, who needs it both for himself and for his relatives. It is important that they do not feel left out when it comes to Victor's treatment. Like Fredrik, they can need some advice about how best to interact with Victor during the time he is in treatment. Fredrik can talk to Jorge about things like this. Fredrik is most accommodating when we discuss all the arrangements.

"I'll do everything you think is good for Victor. Just tell me! Anything and everything!"

"Yes, well, our suggestion is, as we have said, that you come for one session each week for the next two and a half months. This will total fifteen sessions, including the ones we've already had. We'll be seeing you until the middle of June."

Fredrik thanks me again and again, and says repeatedly, "I would never have believed this. The first time I came here I did it because I felt forced to. If I hadn't come, I would've felt guilty for not doing everything I could for my boy. But now I see that I've done exactly the right thing! It feels just right!"

"Well, then, we look forward to seeing the two of you next week, the twenty-eighth of March at three o'clock."

Relieved, Fredrik says, "I'll make it work. I'll do whatever it takes."

Finally, Fredrik asks if I can give him some advice about what to tell the relatives about Victor's treatment. One suggestion I have is to confirm for them that their observations of Victor as too capable and "happy" are correct. I also suggest that they wait some time before reminding him of his mother and Oliver. They should perhaps wait with Victor's visits to the cemetery as well. I encourage Fredrik to explain that the boy will need to use much of his energy in the treatment. He will be on a firmer footing with reality after therapy. It will make him significantly better prepared to face the deaths of his mother and brother. Victor will show them when the time is right.

When the relatives find out that Victor and Fredrik are going to start the treatment, they most probably will experience a sense of relief. Then they will be sharing the burden of responsibility. They have taken on quite a heavy burden and therapy will relieve them of part of it. They no longer need to feel despair when they see that their help is not enough for Victor. They can have some time to focus on themselves. It takes all their strength just to get through each day, one at a time.

CHAPTER SIX

Therapy starts
Session five: 28 March

Gingersnaps make you nice

F redrik comes up the stairs carrying Victor until they are on
the uppermost flight and Victor wants to get down. He
climbs the last few steps on his own with his new navy blue
backpack on his back. Since Fredrik came to the last session alone,
it has now been two weeks since Victor was here last. He looks hesi-
tant as he comes up and he needs a little time to recognize everything. We go into the playroom and Fredrik removes two pairs of
trousers from Victor as well as two sweaters and a jacket. Now he
can move about more freely.

Today there is a snowstorm and the wind is howling outside the
windows. Victor's cheeks are rosy after his trip in the stroller. Jorge
is in the other room, where we have agreed that he will wait at the
beginning of each session. After spending a little time in the playroom Fredrik makes a move to join him. Victor's lower lip starts to
quiver and he looks enquiringly from his father to me, so I suggest,
"We can go with dad into the other room. Would you like that?"

"Yes, I want to," Victor answers.

He gives me a trusting look and seems to relax. We follow Fredrik. Victor trails him like a shadow and wants to know where he is going to sit. When his dad has chosen an easy chair, Victor goes up to it, looks at the upholstery as though he is inspecting it and runs his little hand over the seat. It is obvious that he wants to assure himself that his father will be seated comfortably. Victor smiles at Jorge and, while he obviously wants to stay with his dad, he is also keen to go to the playroom. He starts to pull at Fredrik's bag, which contains his laptop computer. I say aloud, "It looks as if Victor needs to take something with him that belongs to his dad when we go back to the playroom."

Fredrik nods and asks me, "What should it be?"

Victor gives us the answer by dragging the much too heavy bag across the floor towards the door. Fredrik nods approval and I say to Victor, "I'll be glad to help you. If you want, we can carry it together. It looks super heavy."

He accepts my help, smiles and says, "Thank help."

He is quick to see how we can carry the bag together. While we struggle to get it out of the room, he calls to his dad, "We back later!"

He tries to wave with one hand, but realizes that he cannot because he needs both hands to hold on to the bag. He needs to assure both himself and his father that they will meet again in a little while. We leave the doors between the rooms open.

Once we are in the playroom, Victor directs me to lift the bag and put it on his father's half of their shared chair. Then he goes to the easy chair, where all their clothes have been placed, and wants to put on his boots, which his father has put under the chair. I help him put them on. He also wants help to put on his backpack. It is new and looks huge as it hangs there down his back far below his nappy. I wonder to myself whether his Uncle Anton is the one who bought the backpack for him.

Now, donning his boots and backpack, he stands in the middle of the room sizing me up, looking at me cautiously from under his long blond fringe. It looks as if he is trying to figure out if I can pass muster. I assume that he is wondering which one of us is going to take the initiative and start something. I do it by saying, "I really want to help you with different things, like your boots, your backpack and other things. We're here together, you and I, you know, because I want to help you."

Victor focuses intensely on me and I return his glance for a long while. His eyes do not leave me. I feel scrutinized and hope that I will measure up in his eyes. I nod to him to show that I am ready to start our work. I get the feeling that he is expecting me to start crying soon, as all the others around him do when they meet him. He senses, perhaps, that I am indeed deeply touched by meeting him and his father and that I am, in fact, close to tears. I feel the gravity of my task, to complete this crisis therapy with Victor.

His face shows me that he is about to burst from all of his difficult feelings, in all certainty activated by our earlier sessions. I sense that he fears being overwhelmed by his own self and by what he has inside. I want to get across to Victor that I will make sure we do not go too fast. It must not be too much at once. There is no hurry. For a child of the age of two and a half to be attacked by his own feelings can do nothing for the healing process. So I assure him, "We're going to meet many times, all the way until summer comes. We didn't know that before, but now it's been decided. Your daddy wants it to be that way, too. He's going to come to see Jorge. We have plenty of time."

"I go day-care," answers Victor.

"Yes, you do. You go to day-care like before. You come here too, together with your dad."

Victor needs assurance that no further changes of any major nature are going to occur in his daily life.

I try to illustrate the meaning of "plenty of time" for him. Even little children, who cannot tell time, must at least get some sort of an idea of the frames of time and space for their therapy. This gives them a sense of security and a platform from which to work. I put all my fingers in the air since we are going to meet ten more times. I wave one finger at a time to him, talking about all the meetings we are going to have. He looks at my fingers, laughs, and waves back to me with both of his little hands. He thinks what I am doing is funny.

I ask him to come to the table where I am sitting, so that I can show him something. I draw ten little objects on a piece of paper, a boat, a cottage, a man, a tree, a car, a stove, an aeroplane, a chair, a flower, and, finally, a boy. One object for each session, in a wide ring around the paper. I point to the objects, one at a time, and say, "This is how many times you and I are going to meet. We've decided so.

Dad wrote this down in his computer calendar. He knows when you two are supposed to come here."

A two-year-old child like Victor cannot understand time. Even so, the many objects have perhaps conveyed the feeling to him that he will be coming to see me many times, but not for all time. He is so endearing, as he sits there listening and watching me. He mimics me by pointing to the figures that I have drawn on the paper. Victor is trying to grasp this thing about "time", which is naturally too hard. In spite of this, we stay on the subject for a while, so that I can make the point that therapy will be ongoing during the period we have decided. It will not have an abrupt ending, as he might well fear, since the most significant part of his life took such an ending.

I get an almost irresistible urge to lift this brave little lad up on my lap and hug and comfort him with all my heart and soul. I must remind myself that he is not coming to therapy to be hugged and comforted. He gets an abundance of love, tenderness, and solace from his father and many others around him. Victor must get other needs taken care of in therapy. It is important that he gets a chance to work through his grief over the loss of his mother and brother on neutral ground. In order to do this, he needs me to be a person who is outside the contagion of others' despair. He has experienced how others, when they see him, are stricken deeply by sorrow in a way that is too much both for him and for them.

Victor saunters about in the room in his nappy, long underwear, t-shirt, boots, and backpack. This attire seems to serve as a second skin, which he knows instinctively that he needs. He cannot make it now if he is too thin-skinned. He looks pleased and asks, "We gonna play frying pans?"

"Yes, if you want to."

He picks out several of the brown fence pieces that he liked playing with earlier and lays them in long rows in the sand. After a while, he says that they are gingersnaps. While he plays, Victor mumbles to himself, "They gotta stay together. They gotta stick together. They no break, no let them break."

For Victor, nothing is allowed to break.

Before Christmas he had been helping to bake gingersnaps and was told that eating those cookies makes people nice. He wants to make everything around him nice. Then it will stick together better and seem less threatening. He offers me a piece to taste. I thank him and pretend to munch on a cookie. He runs away a couple of times to give his dad and Jorge some cookies. After a while I suggest that he can wait and give them more cookies at the end of our session. I want to show him that he does not have to be nice all the time in therapy. There is room for other feelings as well. Also, he does not always have to be the one who gives. He can and should sometimes be the one on the receiving end.

Victor accepts my suggestion. He puts two small, empty doll chairs in the sand, but does not quite know what to do with them. I just state, "There are chairs like that."

"Yes, we have like that at home," says Victor.

We both know that we are not talking about chairs, but about empty chairs, of which they have two at home now. There are no dolls sitting on them. Nor does he try to put any there. He lets me sense the emptiness as well as his inability to do anything about it.

Victor laughs and I get more gingersnaps in the form of fence pieces. We munch and enjoy the good cookies. He then lines up a number of cannons on the edge of the sand tray. He calls them tractors and is very concerned that they stand close to each other. They stand connected like a long chain, exactly like the figures I have just drawn. While he is fixing the cannons, he stumbles. I am sitting right behind him and rush to catch him. It looks for a moment as if he is going to fall towards a free-standing electrical heater that I have near the sand tray on this chilly day. He does not fall, but his

Figure 3. Two empty chairs are set up and stand alone in the sand. Victor does not see any point in putting dolls on the chairs.
Comment. Now two places at home have become empty, bringing a frightening feeling of emptiness.

whole body is very tense. Before he has even regained his balance, he wonders why I hurried up to him, "What you doing, anyway?"

I take the opportunity to remind him again of the work that he and I have ahead of us.

"I want to help you when you need it. That's why you're coming to see me. I ran to you to help you in case you fell down."

So far Victor and I have only used explicit language about one thing when it comes to the reason for his therapy. I now repeat it again. "You and your dad are so sad. Here we help little boys and dads who are sad. Many boys come here with their dads."

He mumbles something inaudible. I sense that he is wondering if other boys can come in right now, while he is here, so I explain, "When you're here, you're the only one coming to see me. When your dad talks to Jorge, there's no other dad there. The other boys and their dads come on other days."

This is all Victor wants to listen to now. I am very careful to show him in different ways that I respect his wishes. He must get a chance to work through his experiences by playing with dolls and other toys. Verbalizing what he is putting into play will come later. Perhaps he will be able to talk about his mother and brother and use the word "dead" toward the end of the therapy. We do not need to get more explicit at this point. He knows why we are meeting and what we are going to work through. I can feel it in the air that he knows. And he knows that I know what he knows.

Victor is wound up, moves all around the room, and declares, "Can't look out the window. They too snowy."

"Yes, it's snowing a lot today," I answer.

"It okay," says Victor, and shivers.

Maybe he needs to say that it is okay because he possibly associates bad winter weather with catastrophes.

"We're inside in the warmth now," I say.

A big and a little one is gone

Victor wants to reach up to the shelf in the cupboard where the trains and planes are placed. In order to do so he drags a little chair over to the sand tray like he did before and places it on the edge.

Then he climbs up on the chair. I am seized by an exaggerated fear, a feeling that Victor would meet a catastrophe if he were to fall down from the chair. Here I experience first-hand how easily worry and anxiety crop up around Victor. He is not especially high up, but my sense that not a single hair on his head is to be harmed puts me on high alert. He grabs what he wants to play with and starts to fly a big plane noisily around in the air.

"I ride a plane," he says.

Fredrik has told us that Victor once took an aeroplane on a holiday trip with him and Malin. He also went by plane once when there were four in the family. After a while he repeats the climbing procedure on the chair. He knows exactly what he wants this time as well. He picks out a little plane and flies it, too, around the room for a while. Then he takes both the big and the little plane in his hands and flies them around in the air till they crash-land, at the same time, in the sand. He pours sand over them and says, "A big and a little one is gone!"

"Yes," I answer, after a while.

We take a long look at the aeroplanes, now half buried.

After the aeroplane game has ended this way, Victor goes to the cupboard and takes out all the cars. Nothing more is said about the aeroplanes. Instead, he scrutinizes each car and tells its make. When

Figure 4. Victor makes motor noises while flying a big and a little aeroplane. The two aeroplanes crash-land in the sand at the same time.
Comment. Victor often sets up scenes in which a big and a little toy disappear at the same time.

he gets to the hearse, which he has not touched before, he turns it round and round in his hands. It has a clearly visible car emblem in the front, but Victor says, "Not find make."

"No, it can be hard to know," I say.

This car has a strong effect on him. He stands right beside me where I am sitting and puts his head on my shoulder. He starts to speak in sorrowful baby talk that I am not meant to understand. Not a single word is recognizable. Victor turns more inside himself than towards me. I sit quietly, waiting and listening, and the room turns totally silent. He must be left alone for a while as he stands there, leaning against my shoulder. With a faraway look he picks up the ambulance and says, "This a police car. What it doing here?"

I show my interest in his reflections without saying anything. After a while, Victor's attention has turned completely to the wrecking truck and its hook on a string, which is fastened to the crane on its flatbed.

"It has a suspender at the back," he says.

"Yes, it looks like that."

When he picks up the fire engine, he no longer sees it as a fire engine. Although it has a Mercedes star in the front, he says firmly, "It an Opel. Strange."

Although he normally knows most car makes, he cannot identify this one now. He pulls out the fire engine's ladder to its full length and lowers it. Then he puts a little Christmas elf on the ladder. When he is finished, he explains, "Okay for him lie there. He no can walk more. And that car not drive fast. It okay, I think."

"Yes."

Victor next wants the hearse and the fire engine with the elf to be very close to each other in the sand. He complains that he cannot get them to stand close enough together, even though it is impossible for them to be any closer than they are now. He gives up the attempt and gets up from the sand tray. He fetches his jacket and tries to put it on over his backpack. I offer to help him, but he wants to do it himself. Everything gets tangled up and the jacket stays off. He sits on the edge of the sand tray and looks sad. Wearing his boots and his backpack, he cradles his jacket, hugs it for a long time and says in a tender and mournful voice, "My little jacket, my little jacket."

He caresses the jacket and pats it softly and again the room is totally still. I sense that he is recalling how his mother used to caress

Figure 5. A little elf that cannot walk any more lies on top of the fire truck ladder waiting for help. Both the hearse and the fire truck want to pick him up. Victor finds fault with both vehicles and cannot decide which one the elf should ride in.
Comment. In the magical fantasy world of a two-year-old, it is possible to be alive and dead at the same time.

him. It is as if those tender caresses are embedded in his body. Victor regulates things to keep his feelings from overwhelming him. I therefore go along with him when he jumps up all of a sudden and shouts with a joy that is somewhat forced. "Ericabeth, now we play Pippi Longstocking. I be Pippi. You police Kling, no, Klang."

"Yes, we'll play Pippi," I agree. Victor has made up his mind to call me Ericabeth even though Fredrik has explained that the house is called Erica and I have my own name, Elisabeth. Victor knows this but he prefers to put the names together for an all-in-one, so to speak.

Victor looks for toys for our game and pulls out a traffic sign, which he shows me, and wants to know the meaning of. He speaks in a knowing tone that tells me he already recognizes it as a stop sign. He puts it in one of my hands and a police doll in the other. Before we begin our game, I say, "Now I'm in charge of keeping order here and I can stop things so it won't be too much. I'm Policeman Klang and I have a stop sign. That's a good thing to have."

Victor needs to be assured that the psychological frames are maintainable during his sessions. Our play must not get out of control and become more horrible than he can manage. He stretches himself out, beats his chest and sings happily, "Here comes Pippi Longstocking, shola hop, shola hey, shola hop sansa! Here I am! Here I come!"

He remembers that Pippi has a horse named Little Old Man. He finds a white horse and puts three men dolls on him. He also finds the grandmother doll and looks at her. However, she disappears quickly out of his play. He puts his little face into the box of wooden dolls that he has put on the floor and calls right in to all the dolls, "Tommy, where are you? Annika, where are you? They sleeping. Not answer. Can't stand up any more. They gotta be in the box!"

I show him that I am participating in his play by nodding in agreement at him. When he sees me nod, he pulls the queen doll out of the box. This is the first time he shows any interest in a female doll. He tears and pulls violently at the queen's red cloak. It seems as if he cannot stand the sight of her. He is ready to throw the queen on the floor, so I offer to take care of her. He throws the doll at me and I am quick to catch her in my cupped hands before she falls on the floor. While I am straightening out her cloak, I say, "I'll watch her for you. I'll put her in your box. That's a safe place. In the box we're saving everything that's important."

I have put a big box in the room where we can save different things from his sessions. Every child that comes for therapy gets such a box. Victor has noticed many other boxes with names on them on a shelf. I suggest that we write "Victor" on his box. He answers curtly, "I do 'self."

He scribbles a few lines with a pen, where the name is meant to be. Victor does not say anything but accepts that I put the queen carefully into the box. First, I put her on top of a little blue, flowered bedspread in a little bed. Her head rests on a pillow. I thus attempt to give Victor a concrete reminder of my aim for his therapy. I want to help him find a space inside himself where he can preserve his mother and his little brother in his memory. Otherwise he might go through life torn by the wish to throw them away, not talk about them and forget them. This would be so futile. You never "forget" your mum.

When the time is up for today's session, we go and get dad from Jorge's room. Victor brings a whole stack of brown fence pieces and offers gingersnaps to Jorge and dad. Jorge says thanks, eats and

Figure 6. Victor throws away the queen and wants to destroy her beautiful, red cloak. Later he lets her rest safely in a nice bed until it is time for him to accept her in his play again.
Comment. The queen will retrieve her place in Victor's heart, later on.

munches. Dad also says thanks and comes along with us to the playroom, where he starts to put Victor's outdoor clothes on him. When Victor is half-dressed, he goes to the sand tray and picks up two horses, a big white and a little brown one. He lays them on their sides in the sand and pours sand over them till they are almost buried. He wants his dad to come and look at the horses. Dad looks, but does not really see. None of us says a word.

Fredrik has put all the dates for their future sessions in his pocket computer. He takes it out to double-check that everything is correct. Having done so he puts the palm calendar in one jeans pocket and his mobile phone in the other. Then he picks up the bag with the laptop computer that Victor and I have put in their chair. As they go down the stairway they have a little disagreement. Victor, who is tired, wants to hold on to his dad's coat and walk next to him. Fredrik meanwhile is carrying both his own and Victor's bag. The stairs are too narrow and the situation gets awkward. Fredrik lifts up his son and carries him down the rest of the way. Victor is too tired to know what he wants and it looks as if he is falling asleep on his dad's arm. Fredrik truly has many burdens to bear, both physically and psychically.

Fredrik and Jorge have decided that their talks should centre on Victor and on Fredrik's role as a father in their new life situation. Fredrik wants help in understanding his son's reactions. He also

Figure 7.   Victor buries a big and a little horse in the sand. His dad has been wondering how much his son understands.
Comment.   Victor "knows" that a big and a little one have been buried.

continues to meet with the nurse, and those talks centre on his own needs and problems.

Today Fredrik has told Jorge about his younger brother Johan's girlfriend, whose mother died when she was three. She had already told them, before the accident, how sad and lonely it was to grow up without a mother. It seems that nobody had had the strength to talk to her about her mother and her mother's death, and therefore they were not able to help her the way she needed.

Fredrik is distraught to think of what might be ahead for Victor now that he is also motherless. Jorge has pointed out that things will surely be different for Victor. The lad is getting help here and now and the way that Fredrik has committed himself to bringing Victor to therapy is a great part of this help.

CHAPTER SEVEN

Session six: 4 April

Little brother have a daddy?

As they come up the stairs today, Victor is hanging over Fredrik's shoulder. It looks as if he has been sleeping in the stroller on their way here, and has just been awakened. He is sleepy-eyed and his blond hair is wet with perspiration under his cap. Fredrik tries to remove Victor's outdoor clothes but Victor has his own ideas. He insists on keeping his boots on while Fredrik pulls his snow trousers off. He repeatedly refuses to see that this will not work. Fredrik is tired but patient as he explains that the boots are too big and the trouser legs too narrow.

Under ordinary circumstances, such stubbornness, as is typical for a two-year-old, might be expected to lead to a bad scene between father and son. Here is Victor, stubbornly refusing to admit that his father is right. However, Fredrik keeps coaxing Victor to cooperate and after a little while he succeeds. He tells his son that he can put on his boots again as soon as his trousers are off. The weather is getting a little warmer now, but Victor is still bundled up for winter. This might be because Fredrik himself is freezing, inside as well as out.

When Victor is fully awake, and he is so rather quickly, he runs into dad's room, as he calls Jorge's room. He walks up to the chair he considers to be Fredrik's, takes a good look at it and pats the seat as if he is dusting it. His dad gets the message right away and sits down in that very chair. Jorge sits down as well and Victor and I go into our room.

I suggest that we close the doors between the rooms today, and Victor does not object. He pushes them all the way with a little help from me. He runs to the sand tray, stumbles but does not fall, straightens up and regains his balance. He remembers where to find all the toys in the cupboard. In this case, the brown fence pieces, which he takes down right away. Today they become pots and frying pans. He wants to make some food. He kneels on the floor at the edge of the sand tray and cooks and fries his food with the fences. He wants to share it.

"Daddy get porridge. Jorge too. It's good."

"Yes, I think so, too. I think they'll like it," I answer.

He goes to the other room to deliver the food. When he returns, I suggest that he can give them some more after our session is over. I have a feeling that his main reason for going to the other room is to check on dad. To lessen his burden and to show him he can trust Jorge and me to take care of both dad and himself, I say, "Jorge and dad are talking with each other. They're sitting in their chairs, talking about things that dad needs to talk about. Jorge knows very much. I do, too. We meet many dads and little children who come here."

"Well, okay then, I stay here now," Victor answers in a grown-up and matter-of-fact tone.

He seems pleased to be relieved of having to run into the other room. He crawls instead into one of the two closets in the playroom and pulls out a box of wild animals. He is fascinated by the animals, picks them up, turns them round and examines many of them. He gets deeply involved in what he is doing, talking while he sets up the animals on the floor. First out is a tiger cub, followed by many other animals and Victor says, "The first one is little brother to daddy bull. The giraffe is big brother, no, yes. The tiger is his other dad. The horse is little brother, no big brother. Little brother lion baby!"

I take part in this game only by giving a helping hand if an animal falls over, but without saying very much. He continues, "Snake's his daddy and camel other one's daddy. Giraffe is little

Figure 8.   Animal boys together with their animal daddies. "The first one is little brother to daddy bull. The giraffe is big brother, no, yes. The tiger is his other dad. The horse is little brother, no big brother."
Comment.   Victor is working through his confusion about his new family situation. Who is little brother? Is Victor himself a big brother? Does little brother have a dad?

brother, no, yes. Horse is little brother, no, big brother. I don't know. Their daddy and the monkey is thems daddies."

Victor impresses me here with his ability to express in his play his confusion over the relationship between a big brother, a little brother and a father. Who is what among the animals? What is he himself now? Is he a big brother? Yes. No, not now, not any longer. Why? Why not? He selects more animals, which he makes into dads and brothers in different constellations. Finally, almost the entire floor is covered with animals.

"All dads," says Victor.

He gets excited over all the rows of dads and calls out, "All are daddies to two an'mals. Two an'mals are little brother."

I want to show him that I understand his confusion over what has happened to his relationships and say, "It's hard to understand when everything has changed so."

Victor sits absolutely still and asks slowly, out of nowhere, "Little brother have a daddy?"

I am so caught off guard and moved by his direct question that I cannot come up with a good thing to say at all. After a while I just say, in a way that reflects how stunned I am, "Yes, I think you could say that."

The answer sounds strange. Victor does not get what I mean and neither do I. I have not even reasoned my own way through the question of whether a child who dies thereby loses his parents. I thus fail to hold his interest and the theme is lost for the time being. Instead, Victor plunges head first into the closet to see what else he can find in there. He comes out with a little white poodle, saying, "Doggie make me feel better."

He gives me no time to react. Perhaps he notices that he has knocked me over with his clear-sighted and direct question about whether his little brother has a dad now. He finds his own solace in the dog, which he pats and hugs for a moment. I remain seated in deep amazement over how Victor, only two and a half years old, can come up with such probing questions. Is his dead little brother fatherless now, or not? And what about him? Is he a big brother now, or not?

Audi, Mercedes, old geezer's hotrod, and Toyota

Victor needs to calm down and therefore goes to the shelf with the cars. He is on sure footing as he rattles off all the makes, pointing to each car, "Audi, Mercedes, old geezer's hotrod, Toyota."

I start to laugh when, as though it is the most natural thing in the world, he calls a Volvo an old geezer's hotrod. He is obviously parroting something he has heard from his dad. He starts to laugh as well, but he thinks that the Opel make is just as funny to mention as the old geezer's hotrod. I am curious about the old geezer's hotrod and he tells me, "Grandpa has one."

"How do you know?"

"Daddy says so."

"Well, what does daddy think about grandpa's car?" I ask.

"Not good" is the answer.

It would never occur to Victor to question his dad's opinion.

"What do you think?" I go on.

"It's red, of course," Victor answers confidently.

Together we position all the cars in the sand. He tells me which vehicles he wants me to put there. He himself brings out the hearse and puts it down in the middle of the sand tray. He immediately picks it up again, holds it in his hand, takes a good look at it and counts the doors. "One, three, seven, four."

As he examines it, he talks about "the other side" of the car. He puts the hearse to one of his eyes and peeks in through the windows on that side. He tries to see if there is someone in there, or if it is empty. He points with his forefinger right through the window on the passenger side of the hearse and says, looking me straight in the eye, "Mummy and baby gotta sit there. Then they go car, mummy and baby. Gotta have seat belt, mummy and baby. Now we close car door. You get it?"

"Yes, I get it, Victor. At least I think so."

I am so strongly touched by the turn his play has taken that I am struck dumb. He moves up close to me and I put my arm around him. The hearse is still in the middle of the sand tray. We look at it almost reverently. Even though very few of today's children have seen such a hearse in reality, they still know what it symbolizes. Even when they are only two and a half years of age.

When Victor feels that he needs to get on firmer footing again, he wants us to play Pippi Longstocking. Victor has always liked Pippi, but now he truly loves her. He knows Pippi stories and the names of the characters in them by heart. Pippi means something very special to children who, in their fantasy, must manage on their own. She gives them hope that life can still be exciting, even without siblings and with a mummy away in heaven.

If children can be like Pippi, they can be the strongest ones in the whole world and they do not have to be sad just because they are alone. On top of that they will be rich and independent. If they are like Pippi, nothing bad can ever happen to them again. Pippi's ingenuity guarantees that it is so. She can always counter danger, whatever it might be.

Victor is eager to start the game and he naturally wants to be Pippi himself. Today I get to be the two policemen, Kling and Klang. My task is to keep order in a double sense. Victor wants to play this Pippi game in a set way. He tells me to call Pippi.

"Pippi, Pippi," I call.

Every time I call, he rushes out of the closet, throwing his arms wide open, laughing and shouting, "The strongest in the world. Here I come!"

This is repeated many times. Each time I am afraid that he is going to stumble and get his feet tangled in the curtain that is hanging in front of one of the closets. He totters back and forth in a dangerous-looking way but does not fall. He runs to the chair where I am sitting. When he is standing in front of me, we sing together, "Here comes Pippi Longstocking! Shola hey, shola hop, shola hop sansa! Hurray for Pippi!"

The more we sing, the more he finds fault with my singing, one minute too slow, the next minute too soft. He is starting to dare to have his own opinions. He looks at me with the expression of a teacher about to lose her patience when telling me, "Come on! Come on! Give it all you got!"

As he tries to instruct me and correct me, I can just hear his day-care teachers doing the same with him and the other children. I am sure Victor gives it all he has got when they tell him to, because he likes to sing. He knows the words to a number of little songs by heart. He wants us to play Pippi this way many times. We go on singing with gusto, both Victor and I. He thinks this game is so much fun. He likes it when he leaves me and goes into the closet and then we get back together again. He particularly appreciates that it is only make-believe when we cannot see each other. His whole face lights up when I show delight as he jumps out from behind the curtain. Every time he reappears, he shouts, "Hi, Ericabeth! Hi, Ericabeth!"

At the end of the session we go, as usual, to get dad. Since I steered Victor away from running back and forth to offer dad and Jorge some of his porridge during the session, I ask him if he wants to do so now. He runs to get the brown fence pieces and takes them with him to Jorge's room. Jorge pretends to eat and to like the snack very much, and Fredrik thanks him. When Fredrik is putting Victor's outdoor clothes on him, Victor points to the hearse that is still standing in the middle of the sand tray. He wants his dad to look. Fredrik looks, but does not really seem conscious of what Victor wants him to see.

Today, Fredrik has talked to Jorge about how he has asked his parents and in-laws to lie a little low on some subjects, and to wait until Victor asks about his mother and Oliver rather than being the first to mention them. The family have also decided to wait when it comes to taking Victor with them on visits to the cemetery. They understand Fredrik's concerns and his father-in-law has been most grateful for some "guidelines" on how to respond to Victor.

Fredrik also mentions that he is trying to be at home alone with Victor a little more. Until now, someone has come to their home every day to keep them company. Fredrik is making admirable efforts to get control over their drastically changed lives. Malin's brother Martin, who is living and studying in London, has invited Fredrik and Victor to come for a visit this summer. Fredrik gets many invitations to visit and be with others, but, in his present state of mind, he does not have the strength for much of a social life. At the same time, he finds it hard to be at home alone.

CHAPTER EIGHT

Session seven: 11 April

Villa Villekulla is a fortress

W e can hear Victor chirping and chatting with Fredrik all the way from the bottom of the stairs. As soon as they climb the last step, he greets us with a hearty "hi" and, in the best of spirits, marches into the playroom with his father in tow. Today there is spring in the air and it is wet and slushy outside. Victor fell on his way here, when he tried to push the stroller himself, and the seat of his trousers is wet. Fredrik removes all his winter clothes and checks his nappy. He finds that only the two outer trousers are soaked through. Victor makes no objections about taking off his wraps and is eager to start today's work. I hang his trousers on the radiator to dry during our session.

Just like last time, Victor wants to keep his boots on even though he has to put up with being clumsy as a result. He cannot do things in quite the hurry or trot around as freely as he would like. He is endearingly cute in his boots, rolled up jeans and a belt around his chubby little tummy and nappied bottom. Victor looks very much in charge, which shows me that he feels at home and enjoys coming to his sessions. He makes his usual inspection round in Jorge's room, and Fredrik follows him. He takes a good look at his dad's chair and brushes it off. Seeing that Jorge is in his place as usual and ready to talk to his father, Victor makes funny faces at him. Then he addresses the two of them, "Bye now, we go to our room."

Victor takes the closing of the doors very seriously. I show him the red signs on both doors that say "Do not disturb" are clearly visible. The telephone is also turned off. We have important work to do and do not want to be disturbed. He knows that the red signs do not apply to him or his dad. They can go to each other any time they want to. However, Victor's need to see his dad during the sessions is diminishing.

Victor wants me to help him carry cars from the cupboard to his chair. He mumbles and I can barely hear him, but I have a hunch that he is talking about "helping cars". The tow truck, the ambulance, the hearse, and the flatbed truck are the ones he wants us to put on his chair. He sits in the chair where Jorge sits when he is in our room. He keeps getting his boots tangled up in a shawl blanket on that chair. This prompts me to ask, "Do you want me to move the blanket somewhere else?"

"When Jorge sit there, that thing will back."

Victor wants guarantees against changes forward in time. Putting the blanket behind the chair, I carefully assure him, "You're right. This is how we'll have it now, so you won't fall. I don't want you to hurt yourself."

"Okay," says Victor.

"We'll change it back later on. Then it'll be just like it always is. I'll put it back on the chair before you go home today."

This is important for Victor. He may be having some magical fantasy whereby Jorge would change or even disappear if his chair were altered. Who would help his daddy then? He asks as though in passing, "Where's Jorge?"

"Right now, daddy and Jorge are sitting in the other room like they usually do."

Victor seems absorbed in his fantasies, so I reassure him, "Yes, both dad and Jorge are really there. Do you want to go and see?"

He does not want to go, but is content for the time being because now he wants to do some cooking. He takes out a few of his dear brown fence pieces and stacks them on the edge of the sand tray. When he has found a comfortable sitting position on the floor, he starts frying food by pouring wet sand and using the fences as a spatula and stirring spoon. While he is cooking and baking, we talk about different dishes. I ask, "What's your favourite food, Victor?"

He rattles off, "Ketchup, pancakes, ice cream, hamburgers, jam."

I mention his relatives and ask him what their favourite foods are. We talk about how dad likes ketchup and hamburgers, but grandma does not. As he cooks and stirs the fences with a tree, he says, "Grandma makes dinner for grandpa."

"What does your grandpa like?" I ask.

Victor answers mournfully, "Grandma's meatballs. But he not eat. Ever again. He not hungry."

Victor is finished with our talk about favourite food. He gets up and fetches the two little hedgehogs that are standing on the table. He holds them in the open palms of his hands under the glowing table-lamp and says, "Grandpa and grandma. They taking a sunbath."

"Yes, I also think they need warmth. It really feels good for them. They'll feel better later on."

Victor puts the animals at the foot of the lamp so that they can stay in the warmth. I gather from his little narrative that his grandparents are trying to support each other and that they are having a hard time, a very hard time.

It is important to get across to Victor that other times will come, when his dear relatives will be almost like they were before. But that is not possible now. Of course Victor wants them to change back ipso presto. He drops his cooking ideas and fetches the grandmother doll. Holding her, he inspects her from all angles and touches her grey hair. He gives the doll a quick squeeze to his chest and then positions her in the middle of the sand tray. Next to her he puts a stove and on this a doll telephone with its receiver off the hook. He pretends to talk into the tiny little telephone, "Grandma calling."

Nobody seems to be answering grandma's calls, even though she tries to get through many times, so I wonder, "Who's she calling?"

"No somebody. Nobody answer. Nobody home," Victor answers.

He stands up, but his knees buckle so much that he falls to a sitting position on his bottom. He waits a moment before he can get

Figure 9. Grandma makes many calls on the little telephone. Nobody answers.
Comment. Everyone would most of all like to talk to the ones who will never talk again.

up again and then he half-runs to the closet that serves as his refuge, Villa Villekulla.

By this time we have settled into a constructive rhythm during our sessions. Intervals of working through Victor's losses alternate regularly with joyful play periods. He accepts my encouragement to sometimes stick to a theme in order to be able to leave it later. The crucial point of our work during therapy varies from session to session. Today Victor needs support so that too many difficult feelings do not come at once and at too rapid a pace.

When Victor needs to feel solid ground under his feet, he returns either to telling all the makes of cars that he knows, or to Villa Villekulla. This time he chooses Pippi's house and he steps into the closet. He sits down among folders, books, and cardboard boxes, and makes a little nest for himself. He closes the door and wants to be alone for a while in the dim light. He is trying to regain his psychic balance after the game with the grandmother who did not get any answer on the phone. After a while, he seeks contact with me as I wait there on the other side of the door. He shouts, "Ho, ho!"

I ho, ho back. To hear my voice is enough and he remains inside Villa Villekulla. He chats away about all kinds of things, sings, and drums on the sloping wall of the closet. I can hear through the door how he tramples around in his boots on my folders and boxes with papers. He is having fun in the dim light and right now he feels good. He seems to have found a sanctuary in there. My impression is that he views the whole situation of his being here with his father in a similar way. Their therapy sessions have become an oasis in their chaotic life, which must go on in its halting way. Both Victor and his life stumble forward.

Victor comes out of Villa Villekulla after a while and wants to run the trains in the sand. He is ready to throw the grandmother doll and the telephone into the toy cupboard. I hurry to retrieve the two items, take them and go to his box. While lifting the lid I say, "Grandma can be here in your box together with the queen. I'm putting the phone here too. We're saving important things in your box, you know. I'm taking care of them."

We say no more about this because Victor is now absorbed with the engines and train cars. He says, "They're cool. Can hook up."

He asks me to help him hook together the engine and the cars securely in one long row. He runs the train around for a little while but then loses interest in it. Instead, he fetches an elephant and a fox, which he calls the elephant's baby. He plays that the animals are running in the sand, and says, "El'fant runs fast. It not run away."

"What's happening?" I ask.

"Little one wants ride on big one's back," Victor explains.

"What's happening with the big one?"

"It not work. Not work. It fly all the way to heaven."

Victor is excited, laughs hysterically, shouts in a shrill voice and tosses the elephant away from the sand. It goes all the way up to hit the ceiling, bounces against the windowsill and finally falls down behind my desk.

I crawl in under the desk, pick up the elephant and put it carefully on a napkin on top of a cupboard, which will symbolize heaven. All the while I am trying to figure out what I would have done if the elephant had actually flown out through the window up in heaven. It was close. All this is too much for Victor, who goes into Villa Villekulla for refuge again. While he is in there, I speak aloud about Pippi Longstocking, who is inside her villa taking a little rest.

I also add, "She's having a hard time. She's strong, but she also needs to rest sometimes."

"She's tired," says Victor.

"Yes, I think so too."

"She counting her gold coins, I bet", Victor shouts.

"Does she have a lot?" I ask.

"Of course. Three, thirteen, seven, nine," he counts.

"Pippi has many things," I state.

"Mister Nilsson is here and Little Old Man too," a voice says from inside the closet.

"It's good that you have company and that Pippi's taking care of what she has," is my response.

I want to convey that it is both right and important to take care of what you have left. Victor shows by his Pippi game that he is trying to do so. When a child is in Victor's situation, it shows strength when he can be content with what he has left, even if only briefly.

Take away Christmas!

When he has gathered enough energy and courage in the closet, Victor steps out into the room. He has in no way let go of the thought that the fox, which he refers to as the elephant's baby, gets no chance to ride on the big elephant's back. He says in a stubborn and complaining voice, "It want to ride! It want to ride! It must ride!"

With a lump in my throat I agree, "You're right, Victor. The little one wants to ride on the big one. It wants to very much."

"It not work," says Victor.

He starts to laugh and flap around in the room.

"No, it won't work," I say, and look serious.

It hurts to have to answer him like this, but I do not see any other way out. I, too, harbour within myself a strong wish that "the little one could be together with the big one". Whenever Victor plays out his longing for his mother in his games, it is essential for me to affirm and sustain this longing.

He dances around, does stunts like a clown and throws himself on the floor. For a moment I actually feel tempted to put myself on his wavelength and joke with him. Victor makes me feel this way as he goes on clowning, making faces, and looking absolutely adorable. However, to do so would show him that I do not take his longing for his mother seriously. Instead, I say loudly enough to be heard over his noise-making, "Now I want to help you so I'm going to lift you up."

He stops flapping around on the floor and lets me help him to his feet. I say, "We mustn't let it be too much for today. Not for you. Not for me, either. You remember how we decided that I should make sure it doesn't get to be too much."

I sit down in my easy chair and he wants to sit next to me. We sit like this, together in the same chair, without speaking, for a good while. We both need to catch our breath.

Then Victor gets out of the easy chair and drags the little chair up into the sand tray so that he is able to climb up and reach the shelf where the toy boats are. As usual, the chair is unsteady and he is, too. I hurry to his aid because this time he actually does lose his balance and fall off the chair. I jump up on the sand tray's edge and catch him in the fall. For Victor it seems totally natural that I would not let him fall down.

He has never experienced being left in the lurch by adults. As I hold him in my arms he circles his legs tightly around my waist and will not let go. He gives me a hug and I squeeze him back. We are in the middle of the floor and I am struck by how little Victor is. At the same time, it is so easy to treat him as an older child. Indeed, even I must remind myself that he is only two-and-a-half years old.

I let him down on the floor. I certainly would like to keep holding him in my arms but consoling arms are not what Victor is lacking. He is surrounded by many consoling arms. He continues his play from before the fall, stretching to reach the tin boats. He grabs a few and I suggest that he gets down off the chair. It is hard for me to stand there leaning forward, on the alert to help him as he balances on the chair. He climbs down with an armful of boats. These boats have a number of smokestacks. When he is all the way down, he shows me every smokestack and says, pointing with his little forefinger, "This one a daddy. That one a daddy. Daddies and daddies."

He drops a tin boat on one of his fingers, but says nothing, even though it must have hurt a little. Picking up the boat, he shows me the space between two smokestacks where a smokestack has been broken off. Victor always reacts right away when he observes something missing or broken. He explains, "No daddy there. You see that?"

"Yes, I see that. You're right," I confirm.

He starts throwing the tin boats straight out into the room. I stop him, gather them up and put them in the sand tray. I show him that he may throw toys in the sand tray, but nowhere else.

"We can get hurt. I'm watching so that nothing gets broken around here. You mustn't get hurt and not me, either. The toys and other things here mustn't get broken. That goes for everything in this whole house."

Victor gives up on the boats and walks around the room. He discovers the little Christmas elf that he played with earlier. He sits down on the floor and stays there with the elf in his hand. He says softly, "He not see me. No. Not see me."

He gets angry with the elf and tries to pull his red cap off. I let him pull and tear at the cap even though I have just said that nothing is allowed to be broken. It is natural that Victor is furious about everything that has to do with Christmas. He sings some strains of Christmas songs, making funny changes in the lyrics that an adult, perhaps one of his twin uncles, must have taught him. He looks up to them and everything they do.

Victor has a good memory. He knows that he has seen another Christmas elf among the toys and he looks for it now. At the same time he murmurs, "Not see me. Noooo, not see me. Take away Christmas!"

He finds the other elf and says, "Not see, too. Take away Christmas."

Victor hands me the elf, points to his cap and entreats me, "Take away Christmas!"

Victor simply cannot stand to see the red cap any more. I pull hard, take off the elf's cap and give him back the doll. At the same time, I show him that I am taking care of the cap by putting it in his box. He accepts what I am doing because, after all, we have decided to keep important things there. I have a strong urge to protect him against any more stress, like being reminded of Christmas, a holiday that will always have a dark side for him. He says after a while, "Forgot the cars. Oh no!"

He is referring to the cars that we piled up in one of the chairs at the beginning of the session. He lines up the truck, the ambulance, and the tow truck, compares them, and says:

"They alike. All red, okay."

Victor is exhausted and the fact that the cars have different colours does not interest him. His speech shows signs of tiredness but he does not want to interrupt what he is doing. Picking up the ambulance, he asks, "Can you ride in this?"

"Yes, people can ride in that," I answer.

Children in therapy usually like the ambulance. For most it is a symbol of help, recovery and hope. In Victor's case it does not have that meaning. The ambulance was of no help to him or his family.

Our session is coming to an end, and I show Victor that I am going to return the blanket to Jorge's chair. I must show him very clearly that this is it for today. He does not want to leave, so I get up and take his two pairs of trousers, now dry, from the radiator and I open the door. Victor's last move is to put the elephant on its side in the sand and pour sand over it. He joins me reluctantly as we go to Fredrik and Jorge.

Like Victor, I am exhausted and feel like I have run out of things to say. I cannot handle any more today and want to finish the session. It is certainly exhausting to maintain the psychological balance during the sessions. Fredrik says goodbye to Jorge and the three of us go to the playroom, where Victor very quickly grabs a second elephant, saying, "Must be two el'fants."

He returns to the sand tray, puts the second elephant in the sand and covers it with sand, too. As always, he wants his dad to watch. I can tell that Fredrik and Jorge have talked about these parting scenes, because Fredrik's eyes fill with tears as he looks at the elephants. He pats his little boy.

I remind them that the next session falls during Easter vacation. The institute is actually closed then and the building will be unusually quiet. Only Victor and I are to meet at that time. I understand that Jorge and Fredrik have also spoken today about Victor's clothing, which is too heavy for the milder season. Dad chats with Victor, suggesting that they put some of his clothes in the backpack. Victor is very tired, rubs his eyes and does not care about anything more for today. He falls asleep, leaning against his father's leg, while Fredrik is putting his outdoor clothes on him. Before they start down the stairs I wish them a happy Easter, in the absence of anything else to say. Victor comes to and asks, "What's that?"

I just wave goodbye, totally depleted of any more words for this time. I only have set phrases left. Some meaningless well-wishing for the holiday is all I give them. Who cares about Easter? Of course it cannot be a happy holiday. Holidays only make life even harder for Victor and his father.

After today's talk with Fredrik, Jorge is just as exhausted as I am. We are both warmly engaged in these two, father and son, who have been dealt so harsh a blow. During the past week Victor has asked for his mother for the first time. Fredrik says he is relieved because now he knows that Victor has not forgotten her. He had feared this terrible possibility. Fredrik has also taken the initiative to talk about Oliver, telling Victor that mum and Oliver are in heaven. Together they have drawn suns, moons and stars and have looked up at heaven.

Fredrik is now convinced that it is completely right to wait and let Victor talk when he himself wants to. In fact, everyone else has come to the same realization and, as a result, life has become calmer for all of them. Fredrik is amazed that Victor has calmed down as much as he has. He is less keyed up and he is always positive about coming to his therapy sessions. He often asks his day-care teachers about when it will be time for him to go to "Erican" again. He recognizes certain landmarks on the way here and shouts, "There, there" as they come within sight of the Erica building. Fredrik has told Jorge about his decision to take the bus home today, at least a few stops. He wants to test himself to see if he can manage a short bus trip without feeling suffocation or panic.

During the past week Victor had a high fever and Fredrik took him to a paediatrician. Fredrik had also told the doctor about Victor's unsteady walking. The doctor could not explain it, but suggested that Fredrik should wait some time and see whether it might have psychical causes. The fever went down the following day. Fredrik also comments that his own physical aches and pains have subsided somewhat. He thinks this is partly because of the greater calm that everyone, including himself, has with regard to Victor.

CHAPTER NINE

Therapy continues
Session eight: 18 April

Hello, hello, you dead ones!

T oday the secretary calls from the waiting room fifteen
minutes early and asks if it would be all right for Victor and
Fredrik to come up. She senses that the wait will be too
much for them. This time only Victor and I have an appointment.
Jorge is not at work. In order not to let too much time elapse
between sessions, we have set up this appointment for Victor today
even though the institute is otherwise closed for Easter break. The
big building feels empty and deserted. This feeling, and the fact
that Jorge is not here, have put both Fredrik and Victor on edge.

It is important to start and end each therapy session exactly at
the set time, as this helps to establish consistent frames around the
work. However, I can hear from the secretary's tone that they need
to be seen at once. They are both red-eyed from crying, she says.
They arrive instantaneously and, as always, I marvel at how fast
Fredrik manages to run up all the stairs.

Both father and son have a spring cold. Victor's nose is running
and Fredrik coughs as he thanks me for letting them come up
earlier. He says that he is feeling rotten but still wanted to get his

boy to his session. When Victor's wraps have been removed and he is ready, I ask him where he thinks his dad should sit, and he declares, "Bye, daddy! You sit in your room. We in here!"

Today Victor does not feel the need to check out Fredrik's chair. He trusts that his dad can take care of himself for a while without Jorge. Victor does not look well and does not seem to have much energy. His eyes are red and mucus runs down to his chin every time he sneezes. I show him that I want to help him blow his nose, but he turns his head away. I coax him along so that both of us wipe his nose at the same time, each with a separate tissue.

Victor knows, as usual, what toys he wants. He takes out the elephant and puts it in the sand. He looks around on the shelves, finds the grey-haired grandfather doll, and asks, "Where's other one with hair on sides?"

He wants the balding grandfather doll, too. The game cannot start before he has a double set of grandfathers. The doll he means is lying in its usual place, but Victor does not look in that direction. He does not ask for help but makes it clear that he can manage on his own. I say nothing but wait until he finds the doll himself. He also picks up the grandmother doll and lets her join the game.

While Victor is rummaging in the cupboard, he asks about Jorge. I cannot tell him that the institute is closed when the building is obviously open. Nor can he understand about Easter break. All Victor wants to hear is that Jorge is going to return to his dad. I tell him the truth, that Jorge is at home and will be back in three days. While I am talking, I put three fingers in the air to show that there are not many days left until Jorge's return. Victor looks toward the other room and says in surprise, "He not there."

Children often believe that we live in our therapy rooms amidst the sand trays and toys, so I say, "Perhaps you think Jorge and I live here, but actually we don't. We're not here at night. In the daytime we're here. But on this particular day, I'm the only one here."

Victor does not seem to accept what I am saying. He will not let go of his idea that Jorge and I do indeed live here. He drops the subject, content with the knowledge that Jorge will soon be "back home". He continues his play with the grandfather dolls, who are out riding on the elephant, but his play lacks spirit. He is trotting the elephant around at random when he suddenly interrupts the play, throws everything around in the sand, and shouts, "They not want ride el'fant. They want be with them's grandma."

"Yes, I think so, too. I think that's what they want," I answer.

I want to sustain his longing for the ones who are not here any more.

Victor throws sand over the dolls till they are barely visible. Stamping his little foot on the floor he sputters angrily, "They dead! They dead! Dead!"

"Yes, you're right, Victor. That's the way it is."

It is quite healthy and right that Victor should be angry, enraged even, about having been so brutally abandoned. He is able to express these feelings by directing them towards the dolls, not towards those who really are dead and have left him. That would be entirely too horrendous. Victor finds ways of his own that are more manoeuvrable for him. He picks up the nurse doll and tries to twist her head off.

"Don't like her," he says.

I take part without saying very much. He hits the doll, beats and tears at her. After a while I say, "The nurse usually helps children when they don't feel good. She knows how to help. Sometimes it's hard for her to help as much as she'd like. Sometimes children can get angry with her when she can't change things that have happened."

Victor responds by determinedly scraping away the red cross on the nurse's cap and I continue, "She meets many children who are not feeling good. It usually gets better for them after some time."

Victor's response is just to look at me. For children in therapy, the nurse doll is often taken to symbolize the psychotherapist. He really gets to me when he tries to remove both her head and her professional emblem. Although I know that play, as part of therapy, is healing in the long run, I sometimes feel like the brutally battered nurse. It is easy to feel both insufficient and cowardly in the presence of a child as hard hit as Victor. These feelings become especially prominent when he is suffering the most.

Victor goes up to the toy cupboard. While he is standing there, I indicate with a gesture that I want to wipe his nose again and this time he does not object. He really does have a bad cold and he gets more red-eyed and congested as the session goes on. He wants to make some rounds with the trains, but he is too short to reach them.

I get the distinct feeling that he does not want me to offer to lift them down into the sand.

Instead, he wants me to move the entire sand tray so that he can climb up on the lower shelves of the cupboard and reach the trains himself. After pushing and dragging the heavy tray away, I watch him arrange a chair so that he can stand with one leg on it and the other leg on the bottom shelf. This looks quite risky, to say the least, so I position myself close to him but keep a respectful distance. I say firmly, "I'll be nearby so that I can help you if you need me. Only if you need help, you know."

Victor answers just as firmly, "Can do 'self."

He manages his balancing act and gets all the trains down from the shelf, both engines and cars. Victor takes a set with an engine and the cars hooked up to it for himself first, and then gives me a set. He has definite ideas about where the train driver is to sit to drive the train, and he shouts, "Train driver, where are you? We gotta leave now."

He pretends that both drivers arrive after a while. He decides that he and I will drive our respective trains round in the sand tray, along the edges. In the middle of the sand are the grandfather dolls, the grandmother, and the elephant. The idea of the game is for the train drivers to drive their trains round and round the dolls. Victor instructs me, "Both drivers gotta call out same time."

Not really grasping what he wants us to call out, I ask him to explain, and he screams, "Hello, hello, you dead ones! Hello, hello, you dead ones!"

Victor shows me that we are to call out these words once for every time we go round the sand tray. We drive our trains, calling out loudly to the dead ones, exactly as he directs. When I feel that it is starting to be too much, too many rounds for both Victor and me, I drive my train a bit slower. Quick to accommodate himself as he is, he also drives slower, and then puts a couple of railway crossing gates across the tracks. He lowers the gates, the trains stand still and the calls to the dead ones fade away.

As often happens, I am impressed by how quickly Victor picks up the subtle signals that I give to affect the direction and the pace of the play. He seems to sense intuitively how many dark feelings he can deal with at a time. Little children stay sad as long as they can stand it, not longer, and they must have some good times in

Figure 10.   Grandma, two granddads and an elephant lie in the sand. Trains go round and round them and the drivers shout, "Hello, you dead ones! Hello, you dead ones!"
Comment.   The sense of loss is profound when a certain person will never answer you again, no matter how much you call out.

between. Victor seems to know his limits in spite of his cold, which continues to get worse.

He sinks down on the floor, sits on my feet, and leans his face against my legs. My stockings get wet with mucus from his runny nose, but I let it go for the time being. He wants to tell me now about things in his everyday life that have not changed. He talks about what he likes best at the day-care centre.

"We eat 'paghetti. Bake muffins. Go hikes."

"I hear you like going to your day-care. You get good food and you have fun there. I also know you have a teacher named Lotta."

"She super nice," says Victor.

"I've talked to Lotta on the telephone. She thinks you're super, too. I talked to her because I wanted to know how things were going for you at day-care," I explain.

Victor knows that Lotta and I have spoken to each other. She has told him so. He hears that there are many of us who care about him and his father. We talk for quite a while about goings-on at day-care, such as when the children sing loudly, disco dance, and listen to stories read by the teachers. He knows the names of most of the children and can describe the different teachers. He also talks about his grandmothers and about his dad's brothers. It is tempting to let this conversation go on too long, because it makes Victor calm and content for the moment. When he sits like this, on my feet, I sense how obviously and profoundly he misses his mother.

I sit still as long as he wants. I am moved by the strength demanded of me to share his feelings of loss with him. After a while he reaches up and takes down the two small hedgehogs standing on the table next to him. He pats them and says, "They want go on a boat. Want sail."

I take this as a chance for us to stand up. I dry off my legs while Victor fetches two rowing boats. He puts one hedgehog in each boat and makes them move round in the sand. The two vessels are the same size but Victor says repeatedly, "Big and little one sailing. Big and little one going in boats. Do that."

He makes waves so the sand flies out of the tray and both boats and hedgehogs land on the floor. He gets another kind of boat, with a number of smokestacks and says, "I sit first and you behind."

I nod to show that I know where my place is. He points to two adjacent smokestacks that he regards as our seats. Pointing then to the other smokestacks, he says, "Just teensy weensy stumps. They no drivers. Nobody there. Little boat empty. Everyone gone. Noo!"

Here the game ends abruptly. Victor sneezes and does not want to have anything more to do with the boats.

Here comes Pippi Longstocking! Shola hey, shola hop!

Victor takes refuge in Villa Villekulla and pulls the door shut. He does not turn on the light but rummages round in the dimly lit closet, carrying on a little conversation with himself. He is Pippi Longstocking and wants me to call her. I call, "Pippi, Pippi!"

He comes bounding out of the door, shouting, "I'm still here. Still here!"

I acknowledge that Victor is still here and call out time and time again. He answers every time, rushing out of the closet. He delights

Figure 11.   The house of Pippi Longstocking, Villa Villekulla, is a secure fortress. Pippi becomes Victor's faithful companion.
Comment.   Pippi Longstocking is a good model, immortal, strong and rich. She instils hope for an exciting life, even without brothers or sisters and with a mum away in heaven.

in this game and starts to sing with gusto, "Here comes Pippi Longstocking! Shola hey, shola hop, shola hop sansa! Hooray for Pippi! It's me, it's me! Hooray for me!"

A little while after the game has come to an end, Victor looks at me sternly and says, "Where's the rolling pin? You lost it? Shame on you! Find right now. No pancakes for you."

I like the idea of having some pancakes but I have no rolling pin, as Victor says. I help him look for something that could be a pretend rolling pin. After rejecting a number of items, Victor finally accepts a little shovel. He is not so keen on the shovel either, but he is eager to get going on the pancakes. He rolls out the batter, flips it around and lets me have a taste. Today he does not mention that his father must also get a bite. He may be starting to trust that his dad can manage by himself, even though he is alone in the other room today.

"Well, you're going to have a bite yourself, aren't you? You've made yummy pancakes," I suggest.

"No, I not hungry," Victor answers quickly.

"If you really try, I think you can manage one pancake," I persist.

I want to stress that he has needs just like the rest of us if he lets himself get to his real feelings.

"Okay then," answers Victor. "Okay, okay!"

This time Victor understands that I will not give in so easily. He and I pretend to eat a pancake each and we enjoy them loudly. Victor clowns around, sticks out his stomach, and pats himself on his belt. Then he dashes into Villa Villekulla and calls out for Tommy and Annika. He returns just as quickly, saying sadly, "Tommy at his own house. He not here."

He starts talking full speed ahead about Jorge, who is also at his house today. I cannot follow his words, but understand that every-thing and everybody that do not seem to be where they belong upset him. He wants everybody to remain where he or she is supposed to be. It is starting to dawn on him that this is far from the case now. Victor suddenly lunges at me, landing at my feet. Sinking down to the floor, he puts his arms round my legs. He clamps on and says in a tender and cuddly voice, "Little Annika here anyway. Really is. She is for sure. Yes."

I, as Annika, say, "Yes, both Annika and Pippi are here. We surely are. We usually get together. Now we're together."

Victor responds by falling in a heap on the floor. After a while he says, "Pippi tired. She get in and lie down and rest a little."

"Yes," I agree. "I also think she needs to rest a little inside her villa. I'll wait here outside in her garden."

Victor curls up on the floor in the closet and I give him a pillow. The door is open and he talks a good while about a big and a little one. Looking round inside the closet, he sees a big and a little one of many objects and he mentions them by name. There are a big and a little book, a big and a little piece of paper, a big and a little clown doll, a big and a little can of paint, and a number of other such pairs.

Suddenly Victor calls out loudly from the closet, "There she is!"

"Where?" I ask.

It is not easy to keep up with the abrupt changes from one emotion to another. Following him in his search for his mother takes a great deal of my psychic strength. I have come down with a headache and it is difficult for me to think clearly any more today.

Victor calls one more time, "There he is! It's Tommy. Tommy lying there but won't come."

He beckons me with a wave of his hand to join him in Villa Villekulla. There is not much space for me, but I squeeze myself in beside him. I balance in a half-standing position with one foot in a box of paint cans and the other outside the door. Victor, in contrast, is small enough to move about freely in there. I try to get used to the dim light in the closet. He pats the walls down and looks in all the corners. Not finding anything, he pleads, "Ericabeth, help get her!"

Now it is Annika we are looking for. I search as much as I can, considering that I am standing as though in a vice. My headache grows more intense from the exertion. Suddenly Victor shouts excitedly, "Here she is! I found her!"

He cups his small hands and holds them under a paint spot far in under the sloping ceiling. I back out through the door and he follows with his hands cupped. To help him carry Annika, I cup my own hands under his. He lowers his mouth to the cupped-in Annika, kisses her and babbles affectionately with her. Warm air sweeps into our hands.

He sounds like a mother who is cooing lovingly at her little boy. His facial expressions look like a mother's and his gestures are just like a mother's. He shows me, as he has done before, that he remembers exactly how his mother used to cuddle him. This is also the way he will remember her within his body. He will be able to preserve warm memories of her. He slowly moves his cupped hands to his chest and I carefully let my hands follow along. As he holds our hands against his chest, I say, "Yes, she'll always be in there, in your heart. In there you'll remember. We always keep our finest memories in our hearts. That's good."

The room is absolutely still and Victor is calm and at ease. Our session actually came to an end some time ago. I can hear that Fredrik is starting to move around outside the door. It has not been possible for us to finish on time today. Victor must get a chance to return to reality from his play before he leaves. He must do this at his own pace.

Everything feels unreal, almost as though I am seeing it in a film. Victor saunters into Villa Villekulla and starts chatting with Tommy and Annika, who are back in there now. I cannot make myself break up the session. Victor says, "Thank you, help to me."

I am silent. It is entirely too overwhelming and I am totally exhausted. Victor gives me a whole gingerbread cookie, a sand cookie that he baked earlier today. Here he is, a two-year-old, and he wants to thank me for helping him retrieve the memory of his mother. I cannot take the whole cookie for myself, so I say, "Thanks, but I want us to share it. Half for you and half for me."

"No, don't want it. I full."

But now I am clearly more stubborn than Victor and say, "Oh, come on, now! Think about how you really, really feel. I bet you have room for half a cookie in your stomach. After all, we do the work together, you and I. You do half and I do half."

I offer him half the pretend cookie, he accepts it, and we munch on our own halves.

Victor finishes off the session by setting up a little scene from the Pippi Longstocking story using small wooden dolls. This requires a lot of fiddling with the one thing and the other, and since the session is actually over, I help him place the dolls around a table. He lets me know which characters he wants to include. They are the town busy-body, prissy Mrs Prysselius, the two police officers, Tommy, Annika, Pippi's monkey, Mister Nilsson, and Pippi's horse, Little Old Man. We put all the dolls on couches and chairs so that they can eat, because they are having a party.

There are also two small wooden dolls that are neutral, having nothing whatsoever painted on them. They look more like pegs. They are seated on a bench and look like guests of honour. I have seen many children who have experienced the death of someone close to them use these faceless, unpainted dolls. It is understandable that Victor needs to end this session with Pippi Longstocking, who always stays on top of things. As we finish, I remind Victor that next time everything will be back to the usual. When Fredrik puts on Victor's outdoor clothes, he notices that his son's forehead is hot and that he has a fever. Victor goes to sleep before they even get down the stairs.

Today I agree with Victor that Jorge's not being here was unfortunate. I wish I could have talked to him right after this strenuous session. At neither the session's start nor at its end was I able to keep to the time frame. It turned out to be too difficult.

CHAPTER TEN

Session nine: 25 April

Double up with the twins

Today I have to run an errand shortly before the session with Fredrik and Victor, so I pass through the waiting room on my way back. They have arrived in plenty of time. Victor is sitting on the floor fiddling with some cars. Fredrik is standing beside him with one foot resting on a wooden bench. He looks tired and sad. If he takes off his outdoor clothes and sinks into a chair, it may not be possible for him to get up again and mount all the stairs. Victor lights up when he sees me, runs up to me at once, and asks curiously, "You doing here?"

"I had to run an errand. Now we'll go up to our room."

Victor is happy and exclaims to everyone in the waiting room, "We start now. She said so!"

Victor starts climbing the stairs on his own, holding Fredrik's hand. We naturally have to let this take its time and Victor needs to concentrate on the steps and the banister, so Fredrik and I engage in small talk as we go. Fredrik tells me they take the bus to therapy now, round trip. Things are going better and better, especially now that the winter roads are clearing up. He also tells me that his younger brothers, the twins, visit Victor and him rather often. Yesterday evening they had sat up talking for a long time. After they left, Fredrik had a hard time getting to sleep, and that is why he is so unusually tired today. The stairs seem many and long today. Victor thinks so, too, and wants to be carried after three levels. I take Fredrik's computer bag and he carries his son.

Jorge is waiting outside our rooms on the attic level. I put the bag in his room as we come up. Victor gives the room a quick glance while Fredrik turns off his mobile phone. Victor hastily pulls off his jacket and cap and throws them on the floor near the door. He hurries into the playroom and his clothes remain on the floor. He is quite particular about trying to shut the doors tightly between the rooms. I help him to make sure they are secured and he says, "Daddy and Jorge no be disturbed."

"Yes, you and I are also not going to be disturbed. We always put the red 'do not disturb' sign on the door and turn off the phone."

Victor is pleased to see me do this every time he comes. After this is done, he looks around the playroom. Standing in front of the toy cupboard, he gazes up at the play material. I sit watching him from behind and it makes me so sad to think that Victor would have needed his mother for many years to come. I let slip a sigh that I think is soundless. Victor is not looking at me, but he responds nevertheless with a sigh that is also almost soundless.

Little children in difficult situations quickly develop a keen ear for people who mean a lot to them. I sigh some more times during the course of the session and he answers likewise. Everything does not need to be said with words. Much of our communication takes place without words, as is typically the case with little children.

Victor positions himself in front of me, where I sit in my easy chair. He puts his hands on my knees and looks trustingly at me, close up at my face. He is wearing new sandals and a summer T-shirt, striped, in the colours of a football team. He is proud and wants to be admired, so I say, "I see you have a new football shirt. It looks great on you. Please turn around so I can see how you look from the other side, too."

He makes an attempt at twirling round, but he cannot really do it completely since he does not take his hands off my knees. Instead I continue to admire how well his clothes suit him, "You have new shoes too. It looks like your feet feel good in them. With those on, you can walk strong and run fast this summer. Those shoes are just right for the summer."

When I say this, I am thinking of Victor's still wobbly and unsteady gait.

Victor smells strongly of curry and garlic today. I can guess that his twin uncles Anton and Johan made dinner yesterday, when they were visiting their brother and nephew. Now Victor wants us to spend some time talking about things that are fun in his daily life. I, too, am energized by turning a little to fun things. We talk about yesterday and the uncles' visit. Victor used to prefer Anton but now he always mentions both of his uncles in the same breath and he calls them "the twinnies". He no longer makes a point of saying which one is which.

The twin brothers no doubt feel better when they are together in their efforts to help their elder brother and nephew. Victor is happy and excited as he talks about them for a long time and in much detail. It seems that Anton, Johan, and Victor were going to make meatballs but the uncles did not know how to do it. From Victor's happy narrative I gather that grandmother was called for advice. Joking and making merry, his uncles had called their mother "mamma bear".

Victor laughs so hard he almost chokes as he tells me what happened, so it is not always easy to hear what he is saying. His uncles seem to have followed their mother's advice, but what they were trying to make into meatballs turned out to be something else. Victor bursts out boisterously, "Twinnies said mamma bear's fault. Must've forgot something."

He doubles up with laughter and I laugh as well at his rendition of the afternoon and his uncles' telephone calls to their "mamma bear," his grandmother.

"It sounds like you had loads of fun yesterday with the twins. How did the food turn out?"

"No meatballs. All messy. Looked like sloppy joes."

In any case, Victor, with his strong aroma of spices, must have eaten heartily.

"What did daddy think of the dinner," I ask.

"No so good. Twinnies told him eat up and he did it."

Victor does not want to stop so the narrative goes on. From what I can understand, the evening continued with a football game on television and everybody cheered and shouted. Grandmother, who no doubt also needed to hear some laughter, had called several times. Victor gets so excited that he stutters when he tries to make me understand how much fun it was every time she called. It sounds as if the twins teased her and tricked her so that she did not know which one of them she was speaking to. When she asked, they just answered, "Double up". Victor repeats this time and time again:

"Double up, double up."

Every time he says "double up" he puts his two little thumbs up in the air. He is genuinely entertaining as he puts such gusto into trying to tell his story. I have a hunch that Victor grabbed the chance to let loose yesterday by doing all that laughing. For him, that afternoon and evening almost seemed like the times he remembered from before. He wants to be noisily happy, even if Fredrik cannot. I ask myself if this is why Victor was so careful to close the doors and to leave his dad in peace today.

When the narrative has come to an end, Victor goes up to the toy cupboard, picks out the tin boat with all the smokestacks and wants to play with it. The idea is that Victor and his dad are going out to sea in the boat. He puts the boat in the sand and says, "I drive the boat. My daddy sit behind me. I give my daddy ride. Ericabeth sit there. Jorge sit there. Room for him there."

Victor points carefully to the two places that are gapingly empty. He hums like a motor and drives the boat round in the waves of the sea. The sand is flying and the four of us are on our way to some unknown destination. It is obvious that Jorge and I are there to fill in the two empty spaces. Victor seems to have been strengthened by the experiences of yesterday and now dares to move his inner empty spaces into the game. He has specific ideas about how this game should work and he shows that it is important that there are four passengers. He says, "All have to be there."

"Yes, that's what you want," I answer.

It becomes increasingly clear how important it is to help Victor prepare an inner psychic space for his mother and Oliver. Doing it this way, through play, will, I hope, make it easier for him to find the way back to his memories, with all four included inside him. He is right, all have to be there, one way or another.

Daddy's favourite colour is black, but I like red, too

Now Victor wants to drive the trains in the sand. We both work at getting them in order. He takes one engine and gives me another. I hook the cars together because this is too difficult for him. He calls out, "Train drivers, train drivers, come and drive trains! Look they coming out the cupboard. Come and drive!"

We go for a few rounds with our trains and then Victor starts driving his faster and more and more roughly. His train cars fly away all round the room and nothing stays on track. He makes a crash, boom, bang. Then he trips, falls against the sand tray edge and grumbles irritably. He makes some half-hearted efforts to gather together all the train parts, but he soon gives up. He cries softly and says sorrowfully, "Nothing any good any more."

It is tempting to help him fix things, console him and make him happy again. I could at least give him a better train set with stronger hooks, so that the cars would not come apart. However, it is important to let Victor give shape to the fateful accident in his play. So I simply agree that it is hard. "It's difficult when everything's awful and goes wrong and nothing can be done to change it. That makes you angry. That also makes you very sad."

Victor is lying on the floor, his face hidden in his hands. He lets out a little sob, kicks his legs, and slides towards the door of Villa Villekulla. He lies there a while on his stomach and then pulls himself over to the toy cupboard, where he selects two lorries, a red Volvo, and a green Mercedes, as well as two hedgehogs, saying, "These two l'il an'mals be Ericabeth and Jorge."

He puts the two animals on two separate truck beds and then drives them violently round in the wet sand, one truck in each hand. Both hedgehogs go flying and land under the sand tray. Victor complains and criticizes me for not doing anything about all the crashed vehicles, the lorries and the trains, saying, "Ericabeth not help trains and lorries. Naughty Ericabeth. Look, they all broken. They all crashed. Fall on their side. Messed up."

"Yes, they're broken. You're right."

We work for a while on picking up the hedgehogs and towing away the lorries on the tow truck's hook. After that, Victor does not want to play with the lorries or trains any more. He wants to do some colouring instead. He gets some paper and crayons and says, "I make a picture for you, okay?"

"Yes, thanks, I'd really like that."

Victor moves his whole arm as he draws lines both on the paper and outside of it. He makes many thick black lines, but also some lines in other colours. He chats to himself while he draws. His words are not meant for me. He mumbles, "Grandpa, day-care, daddy, Auntie Anna, grandpa."

It sounds as if he is thinking about everybody he knows as he draws his lines.

All of a sudden he says aloud, "My daddy's favourite colour is black. Grandma's too."

He takes the black crayon and colours over everything in his picture. I put a fresh sheet of paper in front of him and ask, "And what about you? What's your favourite colour?"

"I like black, too."

"I see. And do you have another favourite colour?"

"My daddy's favourite colour is black, but I like red, too," says Victor, in a careful little voice.

It seems that he wants to draw new lines with different colours for the different people he knows. However, this is much too hard for a two-and-a-half-year-old. When he has finished colouring, the result is mostly black lines, but there are a few brightly coloured ones mixed in. We talk about how it is possible to have more than one favourite colour, black and red for instance, as in Victor's case. I also mention that we usually change our favourites from time to time.

"Sometimes we like black best and then red can be best of all."

We linger a long time over which colours Victor likes and does not like and why. Black is an important colour for him. He can name all the colours, but is not yet entirely sure about how they all look. He finishes his pictures and we put them in his box. He is holding a green crayon and says, "Grandpa a new car, an Audi."

"What colour is it?"

"Green."

Victor is not very talkative on this subject. He does not mention the "old geezer's hotrod", so I ask him, "I thought your grandpa had a Volvo, didn't he?"

"My grandpa gave to my daddy."

"How do you like that?"

"Yes, no," answers Victor.

Of course he is ambivalent towards everything that has to do with cars and traffic.

The session is finished and we go to fetch dad. Victor makes a half-hearted attempt to lighten up the mood by clowning around. His cap and jacket are still lying on the floor and he kicks them about. He is tired and stumbles several times. It is tempting to make allowances and just let him do as he likes. What holds me back is the thought that if I show Victor too much consideration, then he might do the same towards me. As a result, he would not allow himself to think about sad things or to be sad in my presence, in order to spare me sadness.

I help him pick up his clothes from the floor and I have a serious look on my face as I tap on his shoulder to make him stop fooling around. I want to keep my promise and not let the session be too hard on him, so I say, "I don't think you need to do that any more. Put on your cap because our session is over for today. Now your dad and you are going home together. I'll see you next time. Bye, bye."

Jorge is worried about Fredrik, who was so sad and exhausted that he fell asleep during the session. He has lost weight. It looks as if there is lots of air between him and his clothes. Fredrik had not noticed this himself, but the nurse who is counselling him pointed it out. She has helped him plan a meal schedule so that he will not forget to eat. Fredrik weighed himself and found out that he had lost thirty pounds.

Fredrik recounted his brothers' visit of yesterday. He noted that it was the first time laughter had been heard in their home since the accident. It felt liberating and meant a lot to Victor, even though Fredrik could not join in. He says that three months of pent-up laughter gushed out of the boy.

Fredrik is having a tough time with all the holidays. Easter has come and gone, soon comes Walpurgis night, and then the Ascension holiday, Whitsuntide, and Midsummer. His feelings of emptiness grow extra strong at holiday times. Fredrik tells Jorge what Victor has already let me know, that he has been given his father's car. Fredrik's father wants them to try taking a short drive together, but Fredrik has not made up his mind yet. It is still enough for him that he is now able to face taking the bus. Even though he does not feel quite well, he feels strengthened by the fact that his body does what he wants it to do. More and more everyday matters are functioning again.

Fredrik has a concrete problem just now in the form of a forthcoming outing with Victor's day-care centre. A few of the other children's parents are going to drive the children in their cars. The car trip scares him, but at the same time he does not want to prevent Victor from going. Talking this over with Jorge, Fredrik arrives at the decision to ask his father if he would drive some of the children, including Victor. That would feel the safest.

Both Jorge and I feel great empathy towards father and son, who are now trying together to adjust to their new family, only half the size it was before.

CHAPTER ELEVEN

Session ten: 2 May

My auntie, my auntie

Today, some time elapses before Fredrik and Victor come up the stairs. Victor's Aunt Anna has picked him up at the day-care centre and brought him here to the institute. Fredrik has met up with them in the waiting room on his way back from a doctor's appointment. Anna's little daughter has come along, but Victor has not paid any attention to her. Aunt Anna borrowed a double stroller, where the two children can sit beside each other. Victor had fallen asleep right away and did not wake up until they were inside the waiting room. At the sight of our receptionist, whom he knows well by now, he livens up and climbs out of the stroller.

When they arrive outside our rooms, Victor looks as if he has just woken up and he is rubbing his eyes. He dashes automatically towards Jorge´s room but is stopped by his father. Victor has a messy nappy and needs a change. Fredrik lifts the boy up and puts him on my desk. They both want to get the change over with quickly so they can start today's session. As Fredrik is lifting Victor down from the desk, Victor bumps his head on the sloping wall but seems to take no notice of it. Fredrik looks at his watch. He does not say anything, but it looks as if he is thinking that he has lost ten minutes of his time today. I go to dispose of the nappy and we are ready to start.

Victor is wobbling more than usual when he runs into Jorge's room. He sees that Jorge is sitting in his usual place, greets him, and calls to me in a loud voice, even though I am right beside him, "Come on. Let's go the other room."

"Yes, I'm coming. I'm coming," I answer.

I have to half-run to keep up with him because I want to be prepared in case he stumbles. Time and time again it looks as if he is going to plunge to the floor as he trips and slides along. I sit down on the edge of the sand tray and motion for him to sit down beside me. I want us to have a talk and I explain, "Let's sit here for a moment. Your legs are not quite steady right now. Things were different when you came here today. Maybe that made you tired. Anna picked you up today."

"Her name my auntie," says Victor.

"Yes, that's true."

Victor repeats, "My auntie, my auntie."

"Yes, Anna's your auntie. You're quite right."

Fredrik has made a point of telling his son how he is related to his different relatives. We sit on the edge of the sand tray and chat about some of them. Victor knows who his uncles on his dad's side are and likewise his aunt and his uncle on his mother's side. He also knows the first names of all his grandparents. When he thinks we have talked enough, he gets up and takes out an elephant. He handles it roughly, smacking it back and forth as he runs around the sand tray. I find it hard to concentrate because of my exaggerated fear that he is going to fall and hurt himself.

Victor calms down and starts fiddling with the small houses on the bottom shelf of the toy cupboard. He lines up lots of houses in long rows in the sand, declaring, "El'fant live in all the houses."

"You don't want any house to be empty," I say.

Victor goes on looking for even more houses but finds instead a nice wooden church, painted white, with a red roof and a tall steeple. It is the first time that he shows any interest in this piece, and he studies it from all angles. He groans in complaint when he finds he cannot remove the steeple. He pulls and tugs at it because he absolutely wants it off the building. He wants me to take it off and complains shrilly, "Take it off. Take away, away."

When I show him that it is impossible to do as he wants, he starts to cry quietly. He is next to me, partly lying down, and after a little while I say, "The steeple is stuck there. It has to be like that. The church is a strong house. So is the Erica house. It's impossible to destroy."

He is completely still now and listens as I talk about strong houses and stable rooms. My intention is to assure him that his surroundings here, both the room and myself, are solid. Therapy withstands both inner and outer stress. He needs to be reminded of this, especially today, when his own legs are so unusually wobbly. I take up the topic of church again and say, "Some children believe that the Erica house is a church. There are windows with many colours in the stairway. Have you seen them?"

"Blue, red and blue," is Victor's answer.

I take his response to mean that he has noticed the windows and I am sure Fredrik has. Knowing that Victor's experience of church is the funeral of his mother and brother, I want him to understand that our house is not a church. Perhaps Victor thinks that you can die from being in a church. In that case he could fear that he and his dad, when they are here at the Erica house, can also die. It is so quiet in the room that you could hear a pin drop. We are sitting absolutely still.

To know what is going on inside Victor is not easy, but my assumptions about his thoughts are most probably correct. It is necessary to put words to these thoughts. Victor has stopped crying and is no longer tugging at the church steeple. He puts the church in the sand and says slowly, "El'fant live in church. He feel bad."

"Many children and mums and dads come here to the Erica house because they feel bad."

Victor is listening so I continue, "What's wrong with the elephant?"

"Many years," is Victor's answer.

"What do you mean?"

"Three years," he says.

Perhaps Victor understands that both young and old can feel bad and need reliable support around them. Whether a person is many years old or just three, he or she can need help. I speak again about the many big and little ones who come to us for such help. Victor has seen other children and their parents in the waiting room. To make things concrete, I refer to them and say, "They need help and they get it here. Just like you and your dad."

But now Victor wants to do something else. He wants something from a shelf that is too high for him to reach. He starts a risky climbing venture, which I interrupt by explaining, "Just now, Victor, I don't want you to climb on the chairs. Your legs are not quite steady today. You might fall down and hurt yourself. You remember, I promised that nothing would hurt you here. Tell me what you need, so that I can help you. That's why you come here to see me. So that I can help you."

"Can do it 'self," whines Victor.

He is strong and insistent about what he is trying to do so I make a compromise. He climbs up and I help him a little bit by holding on to his belt. He reaches the plasticine that he wants, takes it down, and wants us to make hot dogs. Victor wants me to knead the plasticine and I make hot dogs in different colours. They turn out to his satisfaction and he says, "Hot dogs and ketchup, yummy, yummy. Come get one!"

"Thank you."

Victor fetches a little toy tree that he uses as a ketchup bottle. He squeezes out ketchup on the hot dogs and pretends to screw the top back on the bottle. He gives me several hot dogs. I thank him and munch away, saying how good they taste. He does not want me to go hungry. Victor is concerned with the needs of others remarkably often. Now I also want to give him something to eat, so I say, "Now I want to give you a hot dog with loads of ketchup. I think you're a little hungry. Please take it and have a bite."

I give him no chance to deny his own needs by telling me that he is not hungry because I quickly hand him the hot dog. He laughs and plays as if he is eating. He wants more and more hot dogs and eats until he pretends that his stomach is about to burst.

When we have finished eating, Victor fetches two aeroplanes. He gives me one and takes one for himself. He wants us to fly the planes, but something is wrong and he interrupts the play. It has suddenly occurred to him that there are only two of us who are out flying. After some consideration he comes up with the idea that his father and Jorge should accompany us. In his play there must

always be four participants. Always four. Victor goes vroom vroom-
ing contentedly around in the air with dad, Jorge and me as passengers. He plays that he is the "driver" of his little toy plane. During
our flight he says, "We go a plane like this one time. But wheel
different. Many round and round."

Fredrik has told us about the trip to which Victor is referring.
The whole family, mum, dad, Victor, and baby Oliver had taken a
trip to great grandmother's place so that she could see the new
baby. Victor can bring himself to think about this trip if he concen-
trates on the aeroplane.

"I know," I say. "Your dad has told me how much all four of you
enjoyed that trip."

A big and a little one is left

Now Victor wants to colour, and I give him some crayons and
paper. He makes lines on the paper and talks, as he did last time,
about how black is his dad's favourite colour. It is also his own
favourite colour, since he wants to be like his dad, but not exactly,
not entirely. He keeps drawing black lines. I make a gesture to indicate that I want to draw as well. He gives me some crayons and we
make small talk about the colours. First he gives me a black crayon,
which I use, and then a yellow one. I ask for a black one again, and
then for a red one. He gets a black and a pink one from me and he
colours with them. We exchange crayons and make a number of
lines calmly and quietly. The black crayons are the ones we use the
most, but other colours are also intermixed. I put the pictures in
Victor's box when we have completed them.

We chat a bit about what colour different things are. Every time
I name a colour, Victor can name several things of that particular
colour. I understand that this is an exercise used at the day-care
centre and he has a good memory. I point out that even if he thinks
black is the most important colour at this stage, it is also okay for
him to prefer other colours sometimes when he feels like it. He
wants to be like his father, but must get help to find the way back
to his own desires. Two-year-olds are always eager to have many
wishes of their own.

Victor is interested in the crayons and wants us to continue colouring. He gets the black and the orange crayons and draws lines on a fresh piece of paper. He reaches for yet another black crayon, and when this one suddenly rolls against a light blue one he drops it immediately. It is as if he has burned himself, so quickly does he withdraw his hand. This is a very intense moment for Victor and he hesitates before he touches the light blue crayon. Then he takes it and throws it, together with a black one, at me. I make lines with the black crayon and Victor says, "Use other one!"

I start colouring on a new piece of paper with the light blue crayon and say, "Look, I'm colouring on a new piece of paper. I'm using this crayon. It's called light blue."

Victor gets keyed up, almost elated, and shouts, "Colour loads more with that one. More, much more!"

He wants me to cover every part of the paper. The whole paper must be light blue. He does not want one single speck of the white paper to show through. The light blue crayon is worn out before the paper is completely covered, but, despite this, Victor insists, "Colour more."

I realize that this is so important that I have to go and fetch some more light blue crayons. I take Victor by the hand and we set out to another room to borrow some crayons. As we pass a restroom, Victor snickers delightedly in the way of any two-year-old. I join in his laughter as we stop to look inside. Victor peeks in, exclaiming, "Look, a toy-a-let!"

I remind him of our errand and we collect the new light blue crayons that we need. Back in our room he continues to insist that I cover the entire paper and nothing less with light blue. While I am colouring, I think of little brother Oliver and I wonder if Victor is thinking of him as well. Maybe the light blue colour reminds him of the little one.

"Little baby boys sometimes have light blue as their favourite colour," I try.

Victor answers excitedly. "Make a big and little one!" he shouts.

I make a big and a little light blue spot.

"Make more big and little," Victor insists.

I make a big light blue woman and a little light blue baby. Victor tells me what he wants, "Big one have 'curry' hair. Little one sleeping."

I put curls on the woman and I make the baby's eyes closed. As I work I talk to Victor, "The big one holds the little one in her arms. The little one has his arms around the big one. The little one is not sleeping. His eyes are closed. I think the big one's eyes are closed, too."

After I make this statement, it feels as if time is standing still. Neither of us moves. The room is absolutely quiet. I have a big lump in my throat. It pains me that I cannot simply agree with Victor that the big one and the little one are just sleeping. Instead it is essential that we approach the subject of death. It is still too early to mention that word, but I cannot let him continue to believe that his mother and little brother are sleeping. After all, someone who is asleep is going to wake up after a while. Victor looks me straight in the eye and says, "Be happy. Make her be happy when she close her eyes."

"Yes, of course she should be happy," I answer.

I draw a smiling light blue mouth on the big figure and, at the same time, my eyes well with tears. Victor notices this, but does not let it bother him now. I am totally overwhelmed by the strength that he has inside of him. He is, despite everything, just a little boy. He is really struggling to get closer to the two who are gone. He takes over the colouring and makes short and long light blue lines, depicting "big and little". He is colouring quietly, without commenting on what he is doing. Does he sense, perhaps, that I need a little respite? He is not the only one who needs to pause sometimes and regain his inner balance. It wears on me to share Victor's longing for the mother and little brother whom he has lost.

After a while, when I am somewhat back in balance, Victor asks again, "Make more big and little."

I do as he says. He decides what the different figures should look like and I follow his directions. The little one should look tired or happy, have no hair, and look around, lie down or sleep. The big figure is to be unhappy, happy or tall, now standing up and then lying down. He watches me carefully to make sure that I do not make the big female figure sleep or have closed eyes.

After a while Victor's speech loses coherence. He is not being articulate and it is no longer possible for me to understand what he is saying. He stutters and is beside himself with tiredness. This session has been quite taxing for both of us. I suggest that we stop drawing "big and little ones" for today. We save all the drawings in his box. When I show him that all the papers are safely placed in the box, Victor says, "A big and a little one is left."

"Yes, that's right! That's for real, Victor. Not make-believe. Not pretend," I answer.

He repeats my words. "Yes, that's right."

"The two who're left are right here, right now. The big one's with Jorge and the little one's with Elisabeth. I'm talking about dad and Victor. It's for real!" I insist.

Five minutes remain of the session. We are both totally exhausted and Victor is about to fall asleep standing on the floor. I put him in my lap and we sit like this, resting until the time for the session is up. No more talking. Today's session both begins and ends with Victor sleeping. I carry him sleeping to his dad, who takes him into his lap. Fredrik asks Victor if he is tired. He reminds him that Aunt Anna and his little cousin are waiting downstairs and that they are going home together.

Victor does not answer. Nor does he hear me say now that he is the only one with an appointment next time, since Jorge is going to be away. Fredrik thanks us for the session, turns his mobile telephone back on, and carries his sleeping son down the stairs. Victor looks heavy and Fredrik's back hurts. I notify the receptionist, who is near the waiting room, and she asks Aunt Anna to start up the stairs and meet the two half-way.

Yes, Fredrik's back has been hurting. He has been to the doctor today for an emergency visit and the diagnosis is a slipped disc. The doctor, who did not know anything about Fredrik's traumatic experience, had said that a slipped disc can be triggered by psychic stress. When the doctor asked Fredrik if he was stressed, Fredrik did not feel like being open to him and answered in the negative. He thought to himself that the doctor was the one who was stressing around far too much. Fredrik tells Jorge that he sometimes must keep quiet about his losses to protect himself from other people's reactions.

Most people cannot bear to hear him tell what has happened to him. Many act strangely, Fredrik finds. They do not greet him or they avoid him, saying nothing. He says that the most forthright people are the children at Victor's day-care centre. They ask where Victor's mother and little brother are, and when Fredrik answers that they are dead, they take it well. Some children have posed this question several times. Fredrik has noticed that if he answers them directly, they do not ask Victor as much.

Fredrik has also told Jorge that he would like to go away for a day and a night with a friend. Jorge advises him to prepare Victor very carefully. Fredrik says that he has already done so. It has been decided that Victor's maternal grandparents, Aunt Anna and his little cousin will all stay at home with him while his dad is away. Before the accident, Victor's grandfather had been the one to take care of him when his parents were away. But now the grandpa and grandma want to be there together with Anna.

CHAPTER TWELVE

Session eleven: 9 May

Magical thoughts

As previously arranged, Victor and I are meeting as usual today, even though Jorge is not here. When I wanted to prepare Victor for this change at the end of the last session, he had already fallen asleep. However, Fredrik has told him that Jorge will be away today. Victor is joking and calling out my name in a whisper from far below on the stairs and I greet him in return, in the same sort of mock whisper. His dad carries him into the playroom and puts him down on the floor. Victor holds his hands cupped over his mouth as if stifling a laugh. Fredrik does not want to disturb us and says that he will sit and wait in a room next door.

I lead the way and show Fredrik a room they have not been in before, while Victor comes bouncing after us. He wants to see how the room looks where his dad is going to wait for us. It now seems more of a habit than a need for Victor to check out Fredrik's whereabouts. After a quick glance at the room, he says, "Bye now. We leave now. We go our room."

I also say goodbye to Fredrik and follow Victor, who asks about Jorge on our way into the playroom. He poses many questions at the same time, but without the same intensity as earlier.

"Where is he? Why not here? When he coming back?"

I give him straight answers. "Jorge is at home. He'll back for your dad's and your next visit."

I have told him before that we do not live in our therapy rooms, but he still wants it to be that way. He needs me to let him believe that we can always be found here, so we do not expand on this any more now.

All of a sudden someone knocks on the door. I open it and say that I am busy because I have a visitor. I notice that I have forgotten to turn the red "Do not disturb" sign around. Victor wants to do so now, to make everything as usual. I lift him up so that he can reach the sign and turn it around. When he has done so, he says, "This is our at home, Ericabeth."

"Yes, you feel at home here. You like to come here to meet with me. I can see that."

Victor says as though no one could deny it, "We live here."

"I'm here every time you come. I'm waiting for you. We're here together."

Today the sand tray is still covered. I usually remove the cover and put it next to the tray before Victor comes in. I have had a hectic morning right up to the time of Victor's arrival, and I have forgotten the cover as well. He does not waste a minute. He goes up to the sand tray, looks sternly at the cover and asks, "Who put that thing on there?"

"Yes, that's not the way it usually looks, is it?" I say, vaguely.

Victor does not wait for me to be more precise. Instead, he comes up with his own explanation, "Jorge did it. He here to fix it. I know he do."

He is standing with one hand tucked under his belt and looking stern as he lets me know of his disapproval. He is determined to make me understand that he does not want any more unexpected changes. It impresses me how he makes the situation clear for himself by finding an explanation. Via some magical thinking, he attributes energy and actions to the one who is absent. At the same time, he shows that he dares to think about and remember someone who is gone. Right now, Victor needs to hear one more time that Jorge still exists, even though he is not at Erica House at this particular time.

"You wonder, perhaps, what Jorge does when he's not here? You can't see what he's doing now," I say.

"What he do?" Victor wonders.

"Well, actually, I don't know. I can't see what he's doing, either. Maybe you also wonder what other people do when they're not together with you?"

Victor flops on his bottom on the floor. He listens intensely for a while, but does not comment on anything I say. I get the feeling that this topic must be given a chance to sink in. By turning his nappied rear end towards me as he pulls himself up off the floor, he shows me that he has had enough for now.

Instead, he wants to play and be happy. He throws toys around in the sand tray, making sand fly all over the room. The sand ends up being spread over the floor and I let it go for the time being. It crunches under our shoes when we step on it, but it warms my heart to see that he feels like being a little mischievous.

Victor tries to jump with both feet together on the part of the floor where most of the sand has ended up. This calls for a skill that is too advanced for a two-and-a-half-year-old, but he thinks he is just great at it. We both laugh at his attempts to coordinate his legs and feet as well as his new sandals as he jumps. He is less unsteady today, but falls nevertheless time and time again. When he gets tired and wants to rest, he says, "Jorge be mad about sand on the floor."

"How do you mean?" I ask.

"Ugh, it's messy! He not like it. Shame on you!"

It is clear that Victor attributes to one who is gone such characteristics as mothers usually have. He is well on his way to daring to open up for more concrete memories of his mother; what she did, what she said, what she liked and did not like. For this he must be given the time he needs and must not be pressured. To make it bearable, he takes the route via Jorge and attributes his mother-related thoughts and feelings to him.

His interest in the topic fades and he wants to turn to something less emotionally charged. He has quite a knack for finding everyday things in the room to use in an imaginative way. Before play can go on, however, he wants to do something about his shoes. He sits down on the edge of the sand tray to brush the sand off the soles of his sandals. He repeats this several times and every time he puts his foot back on the floor, the sole gets covered with sand again. He shows me the soles of his shoes and thinks he is showing me the shoes in their entirety. I admire his sandals, the top of them, the bottom of them and all around, saying, "They look like excellent jumping shoes. They fit your feet so well. You can do loads of jumping in those shoes this summer."

"Yes, I think," he answers.

I open the window and leave it ajar to let out some of the dust that all his jumping in the sand has produced.

Help to me

Victor fetches some plasticine, sits down on the sandy floor and begins to knead. There are several colours of plasticine, but he chooses only the light blue one. The plasticine is hard and he asks me for help. "Make a big and a little thing! They be alike."

"Okay, sure. Tell me how you want them to look."

He motions with his small hands to show me. I knead the plasticine in the way I think he means, making a big and a little ball, which I hand to him. He climbs into the sand tray with a shovel in his hand. There he pours sand first over the big ball and then over the little one. He pulls them out from under the sand and then buries them anew. He repeats this again and again and says at the same time, "A big and a little one. A big and a little one."

Victor gets discouraged because he wants there to be an exact amount of sand on the balls. It saddens him when he is unable to cover them the way he intends; that is, with exactly the amount of sand that he has in mind. Struggling with his shovel, the sand, and the balls, he sighs deeply several times, after which he turns to me and says irritably, "Help to me! I can no dig down the big one. It shows all time."

The air in the room is filled with tension during this burial work. Victor throws the shovel at me and I pick it up. He whimpers in frustration at his helplessness. I can feel a headache coming on as I face the thought that Victor, symbolically in his play, is asking me

Figure 12.   Victor tries to bury a big and a little ball. He has a hard time decid-
ing whether to put a thick or a thin layer of sand over them.
Comment.   Is it possible to remember the buried ones? If you see them? If you
do not see them?

to help him so that his mother and little brother can disappear to
just the right extent, not too much, not entirely.

Victor wants everything to be done in a very particular way and
tries to give me instructions. No matter how hard he tries to show
me what to do, it does not turn out the way he wishes. But can there
ever be a good enough way to do what we are doing? Although it
feels so difficult, I must bring myself to assist him properly in this
burial game. It is my task to help him remember and to retain the
memory of his mother and little brother as they were when they
were alive.

I go and get another shovel and now we each have one. I let him
choose whether he wants us to work separately, each with our own
shovel, or together, with the same one. He points to the one that is
blue and says, "We take green one."

He crawls into the sand and sits down next to the plasticine
balls. He takes a firm grip on the shovel and I cover his hand with
mine. We pour sand over the little ball first. We stop when there is
as much sand covering the ball as Victor wants. Then we start the
same serious process of pouring sand over the big ball. We pour
until Victor shouts, "Now too much. Can't see her."

He takes the two balls out of the sand and we try many times with both our hands on the handle of the blue shovel. This is a difficult task in every way, especially with regard to the big ball. We end up with either too little or too much sand over that one. After a long while and many attempts, I am exhausted from the tension, and I note that Victor seems to be so as well. I suggest, "Now let's try for the last time for today. Let's pour the sand slowly, both you and I, and watch for when there's the right amount on top of the balls. I'll help to decide."

Victor seems relieved and, after pouring a number of times, he says in a tired voice, "Enough. Now's enough."

I concur. "You're right. This is enough for today."

The plasticine balls remain in the sand, half-buried. Covered with sand from head to toe, Victor climbs out of the sand tray. He moves close to me, leans against me for a while, and says, "Let's go Villa Villycoolly."

"Yes, let's do that! I think we need a little rest," I answer.

Victor, who does not want to rest, says, "Balls come along to Villycoolly."

"Okay but then we'll move them together. Let me help you," I insist.

I carry the big plasticine ball carefully and Victor the little one. He grabs the elephant on the way and explains, "El'fant live here. Not alone. Little one live here with him."

"Yes, a big and a little one live together in the villa," I say.

It is important for Victor that nobody lives alone. We enter Villa Villekulla together and put the balls on a shelf in the closet.

The closet is messier than ever, so I have an even harder time getting in now than previously. There is no bare floor space left where I can stand, but I squeeze myself in next to Victor and manage to fit halfway. He wants to close the door of Pippi's house and tries to do the impossible, tugging impatiently at the closet door. When something keeps stopping him, he looks around and discovers that the obstacle is my left leg. He scolds the leg and squabbles with it as he tries to lift it into the closet. He says, "It too big. Take it away. Close the door."

He huffs and puffs as he tries to move my leg and his face gets redder and redder. Finally, I cannot help bursting out in laughter at his utter determination. I lose my balance and he finds it extremely funny when I fall to my knees and turn over the box full of wooden dolls. He laughs long and gleefully as he watches the dolls roll all over the floor. I grimace and make faces until I get on my feet again. Victor thinks it is all hilarious and I suggest, "Let's pick up the dolls together and get them off the floor. Otherwise we'll slip on them."

Victor goes on laughing and tries to convince me to continue the confusion.

"Fall down again. Again! Not pick up."

He sits on the floor laughing while I crawl around picking up the dolls. He goes back to his play about Villa Villekulla, which was interrupted, calling. "Annika, where are you?"

Sensing that he wants me to be Annika, I answer, "I'm here. Where's Pippi?"

"I'm here," he answers.

As always, Victor wants to be Pippi. Now he starts to wonder about Tommy's whereabouts. He calls out to him and I ask, "Where do you think he is?"

"Tommy's no place. He resting. We all alone now," Victor states.

"There are two of us left here," I affirm.

I take part in the play without saying much more and Victor continues, "We fix this. Here's our house. We take care of it. We make Villycoolly nice."

Now Victor starts a big cleaning project. He sweeps and brushes off things in the closet, kicking aside the objects that are covering the floor. He looks at the plasticine balls on the shelf and lets them be. In his play Victor puts together a new home that is big enough for two people, no more, no fewer. One moment it is for Pippi and Annika, the next for himself and me. I can see that he is trying to adjust to his new reality, to being part of a family of two, and I want to support his efforts, so I say, "Victor, you're absolutely right. It's great that you're cleaning up and changing things around so that it fits two people."

When Victor has finished cleaning up in the villa he stretches one foot towards me. He points and shows me that he has sand in his sock and between his toes. I remove his shoes and socks and pour out the sand. He wiggles his toes while I brush away the sand from his little feet. When his socks and shoes are on again, I notice that he is somehow still focused on his shoes. To gain time, since I do not understand what his wishes are, I praise his sandals again.

I wonder if his uncles bought them for him, but I keep my thoughts to myself. In a tone of distress, Victor answers the question that I have not asked aloud, "Nobody buyed them."

It appears that both of us, at the same time, have been thinking about where the shoes come from. I assume he means it was not his mother who bought them. She was the one, after all, who always used to buy clothes for him. I have no other choice but to confirm that he is right.

"You're right. Things are not like they used to be."

He strides over to the toy cupboard and picks out a broken car, which we repair with tape. We note that the door on the passenger side is broken and we use several layers of tape on it. What we have done is meant to keep the car door in place. Victor pokes around and picks at the tape and says suddenly, "My mum sits in there."

"Yes, she does."

Victor talks to himself, mumbles and speaks unclearly. It sounds as if he is making up his own words, intended only for himself. He repeats what he says many times and I nod to show that I am with him. Victor is showing clearly that right now he wants to talk only to himself. He has moved away from me on the floor. He senses perhaps that my greatest urge is to put him in my lap and hold him and he does not want that now. He peeks in through the taped car door. I pick up that he is talking about a big and a little one named something like "Mazsp" and "Xyzmk". He is totally absorbed in his thoughts and as he touches the car he mumbles in a low voice, "I want be near."

Any comment from me seems superfluous. It is enough just to be near him right now. My hope is that Victor will be able to feel this nearness to his mother inside himself and at the same time, go on with his life.

When the time is up, Fredrik knocks lightly on our door. Victor runs to open the door, shouting, "We've been in Villa Villycoolly."

He thinks it is fun to call Pippi's house, Villa Villekulla, by the name Villycoolly.

"Look. We've tidied up everything."

The room looks anything but tidy, so his dad smiles and says that Victor looks like a sandman. Fredrik brushes most of the sand off of Victor and says that the rest has to wait for his evening bath. In the meantime, I fetch the two plasticine balls from the closet and put them with the repaired car into Victor's box for important things. Victor shows his father the balls and Fredrik, not knowing what they represent, says, "Very nice."

Before they leave, Fredrik asks me whether Victor walks more steadily now than during earlier sessions. At home he almost never stumbles any more. I agree that he is steadier and keeps his balance better. Fredrik also tells me that his overnight stay away from home went well. It was, however, easier for Victor to be without his dad than for Fredrik to be away from Victor. He says that he thought about Victor every fifth minute and wondered how he was. He thought about how Victor was at home without any parent. He thus has made a decision not to do anything risky. If something were to happen to him, Victor would be an orphan. Fredrik and a friend of his used to have fun scuba diving but now Fredrik has lost interest in it.

CHAPTER THIRTEEN

Session twelve: 16 May

Dad in his own need is grateful

Today, Fredrik visits me alone to hear how Victor's healing process is going. The only appointment time I have been able to offer him is after the end of the working day. Fredrik is early and has made himself comfortable in the waiting room, which is empty this time of the day. After I fetch him and we go into my room, the first thing he tells me is that his brothers have picked up Victor at day-care today. They are taking care of him while Fredrik is here and right now they have gone somewhere to get a hamburger.

Victor had spoken with his uncles on the phone yesterday about how much fun they were going to have. With dad's help, he phoned Anton first and then Johan. Fredrik laughs in amusement and is somewhat surprised at the way Victor is able to take on the family style as far as manners are concerned. Victor, he points out, now sees the twins as two separate individuals, even though he calls them "the twinnies". Victor loves being with them and Fredrik says, "You know, they're the ones I can count on the most. They're the only relatives who can manage to keep their spirits up, at least somewhat. Well, I guess that's the good thing about being twins, isn't it? They're used to volleying with each other's mood swings. When Johan is down in the dumps, Anton usually cheers him up, and vice versa. Victor looks up to both of them and likes it best when he is on his own with them."

Fredrik says that he has looked forward to our talk today. Many things about Victor astound him. He wants us to focus especially on the changes in Victor's behaviour and says in amazement, "Victor really knows what's going on here. I notice how eager he is to start when we arrive. He wants me to disappear with Jorge as fast as possible, preferably behind closed doors."

I agree, by saying that during the sessions I, too, notice that therapy is important for Victor.

"Can children as little as Victor feel a need for integrity? Already, that young?" Fredrik asks.

"Yes, Victor needs to work through his grief in his own way, in peace and quiet. By closing the doors he arranges things so that he gets what he needs, a space of his own. He needs to trust that he can have a space to express the feelings he has, sorrow, despair, anger, and sometimes even joy. It's important for him to feel that it's also okay to be happy during therapy."

Fredrik is listening and I continue, "I think it's hard for Victor to be happy for even a short while, when he sees you're sad. That's also a reason why he's so careful about shutting the doors."

I tell him that little children grieve a little bit at a time in therapy and stop before it gets to be too much, provided that they are well taken care of.

"Is that so? I didn't know that, it never occurred to me. Well, it's lucky they do it that way. Of course, that's the way it has to be, I guess. How could they stand it otherwise?" Fredrik says.

It is therefore necessary to establish a rhythm in therapy between themes that evoke different feelings. This is true for Victor's therapy as well, and I explain further. "I always try to balance the session so that it will not be too much for him. The painful topics cannot be allowed to dominate, nor can the playful activities. Victor fluctuates between being sad, angry, happy, and the good, clever boy who can manage everything. With time, Victor's become clearer and clearer at showing when he needs to change the scenario."

"I don't know if you remember, but in the beginning I was afraid it would really crush Victor if, via therapy, it dawned on him all too suddenly what has happened to us. As it turns out, therapy has not led to anything like that, not at all. On the contrary," says Fredrik.

I say that I remember Fredrik's fears, and he continues, "It's as if reality comes to him in small child portions. He absorbs a little bit at a time, so to say. It's damned tough for a two-year-old. But my parents say that, despite everything, this must be the right way to go. I think so, too.

We sit quietly for a while. It moves me as I think about Fredrik's use of the words "child portions". I take that as a solid compliment on our work, for both Victor and myself. Fredrik does not know how to express it, but in his own need he is very grateful for the help that Victor is getting. His feelings of gratitude overwhelm him and he says, "Words just can't express what I feel. All words just fall short."

After a while we go back to where we left off, talking about concrete events in Victor's life. Fredrik tells me about a recent incident that took place when Victor visited his Aunt Anna and his little cousin. Anna had overheard how Victor was telling his cousin, who was lying there in her baby carriage, that his mother and Oliver were dead. His cousin is one year old. To get her attention Victor had clapped his hands in front of her eyes. She had answered "da, da, da", and Victor had replied that it was really true.

When Victor noticed that Anna was crying he did not console her, which he would have done earlier. He had instead been able to accept the solace she gave him. He sat still in Anna's lap and listened as she explained that she was crying because her sister, Malin, was dead. They had spent considerable time on the fact that Malin was Anna's sister. The more Anna tried to explain, the more confused Victor became. Finally, Victor had let her convince him that the two were sisters when they were little, but he refused to believe that it was so now, because Anna is, after all, his auntie.

Later in the evening, at the dinner table, where Fredrik and Malin's dad were present as well, Victor had said out loud, "My mum's dead and so's Oliver." That made it possible for them to speak about Malin, at least for a little while. The family had been so relieved when Victor did not start laughing or clowning around. All of them felt in somewhat less of a gloomy state after this. Victor's grandfather expressed the relief that everyone felt when he said, "It's comforting that the lad didn't go crazy. It seems like he understands and he's going to be okay." The mere thought that Victor could be expecting his mother to return home has pained them all severely. Fredrik asks me, "Do you think Victor will take anything at all of Malin with him through life?"

I tell him what I believe. "I see in Victor a little boy who has received lots of love from his mother. This has made its imprint on him for life and has given him a large dose of basic trust. He'll always take that with him. Children who have received good care early in life build up an inner psychic stability."

Fredrik wonders, "How can you be so sure of that when it comes to Victor?"

"He's so trusting. That helps him to benefit greatly from his therapy", I explain, and continue, "As a child psychologist, I meet many children who for various reasons have not had as good a childhood as they should have. Working with these children has given me a broad experience of the consequences that an insecure childhood may sometimes have. I can say with the greatest conviction that a loving sense of security is one of the best things you can give a little child."

I ask Fredrik whether Victor most resembles his mum or his dad. Fredrik says immediately and without reservation that Victor is most like Malin. He is cheerful and sociable by nature. He talks a lot, like his mother did. Fredrik adds, "I'm impressed by Victor's talents. Myself, as I remember it, I was a more sullen and standoffish type as a kid. What I liked best was to make myself a little tent or jump on my bike and go off with the lads in my neighbourhood."

Fredrik comments several times on how amazed he is that therapy has helped Victor so much. He returns to the doubts he felt at the outset, which were grounded in his fear that I would find some serious psychological damage in Victor.

"I mean, he escaped from the accident without any physical injuries at all, so I just couldn't stand the thought that there might be something else wrong with him. I was clinging to the idea that Victor had to be totally okay."

Fredrik has spoken with Jorge concerning these feelings and perceptions about his son and he says, "It would be terrible if Victor felt he had to go through life being perfect for my sake, that I'd be devastated otherwise."

Fredrik lets me know that through his talks with Jorge and the nurse he has come to realize things that had never even entered his mind before. He struggles to understand what is really behind what Victor is trying to say, but it is not always so easy. Fredrik is also realizing more and more that with little children words are not always the most important things.

He recounts, "Whenever Malin heard the slightest peep from either of the kids, she knew what just that particular peep meant, just that particular time. Me, I tend to use some kind of process of elimination, so to say. I go through a mental checklist of everything that could be the matter, like is Victor hungry, does he need a nappy change, does he have a cold?"

We talk a little about mothers' and fathers' differing relationships to their children. Fredrik sadly expresses the fact that he now has to be both mother and father to Victor.

But I'm here with you, daddy

To show Fredrik how Victor is working through his grief, I give him some examples from our therapy sessions, including the time when Victor ended by burying two animals in the sand. He was eager to show Fredrik this scene before they left to go home and I say, "I see this action as Victor's attempt to show you that he knows. A burial scene is something the two of you have shared. He's more interested in showing this to you than to me."

Fredrik listens and wants to hear more, so I go on. "When I observe what Victor does during the sessions, I see three recurring and consistent themes: *disappearing*, *searching*, and *finding* or *not finding*. We call out for toys that are out of our view. Sometimes he wants to find them and sometimes he wants them to remain lost."

I also tell Fredrik about Victor's delight in Pippi Longstocking. She's not only a storybook character to him. She's his idol, his heroine. He looks up to her and wants to be like her, wants to be her. I see it as a good sign that he chooses such a life-affirming character as a model. If you're like Pippi, you'll get along just fine.

Victor is also working through his trauma by staging car crashes.

"We repair broken cars with tape so that nobody can fall out again."

I also tell Fredrik that I have a hard time grasping how much Victor really experienced of the violent impact of the crash. He may have been asleep during most of the time that elapsed before help arrived.

"How can we find that out?" asks Fredrik.

"I don't think we can, for now. It can become clear with the passage of time. In many cases it takes a long time before children retrieve such frightening memories. Maybe he was sleeping, but you know, even in that sleep he experienced the collision. More exactly what he experienced and what he has in his body memory may surface later on, but not necessarily."

I continue, "Victor has preferred to have four participants in his fantasy play, just as many as used to be in his family. Recently, he's also started to set up play scenes involving two people, which is the size of his present family. This way he shows he understands more and more about how his family has changed."

"It's just too dreadful, all of it. But I do feel more at ease now that it's okay to show sadness in Victor's presence," Fredrik says.

He is following Jorge's advice to let Victor know that he gets sad when he thinks about Malin and Oliver. That way, when dad is sad, Victor does not have to get the idea that another catastrophe has taken place. Fredrik has also understood that it is important to tell Victor when he feels less sad. He says, "His eager efforts to console me are really moving. Now it's more that we console each other, taking turns when one of us is particularly sad."

Fredrik adds, "I understand that I have to be clear in letting him know that I'm still the adult. I'm the one to make the decisions and to take responsibility for everything."

We note that this holds true even when Fredrik is feeling sad. Before the accident, his adult role and responsibilities were automatic to him. It never even crossed his mind that things could be otherwise. Fredrik notices that the clearer he is, the calmer Victor becomes. He also says, "He has stopped all that compulsive stuff where he felt he had to do something funny every minute. He isn't so wound up and he doesn't clown around."

One evening, when Victor saw Fredrik crying, he patted his dad and said, "But I'm here with you, daddy."

"Well, you can't go on crying very long when Victor says that, you know," comments Fredrik.

A little while later, when Fredrik found Victor crying, he consoled him with similar words, saying, "But I'm here with you, Victor."

"Yes, I see how you two are good at consoling each other."

Fredrik has told me earlier, but he mentions again, that the two of them now take the bus to and from therapy. He is relieved that he can manage this trip in a problem-free way. He has also driven the car that his father gave him. It was only for a short distance, but it took a lot out of him.

We are getting closer to the end of therapy, with only three sessions to go, and we talk about what this means. Fredrik wonders, "What am I going to say to Victor if he doesn't want it to stop? What if he says he wants to come some more times?"

"It's never easy for children to end therapy. To prepare for a good conclusion is one of the most important parts of the therapist's work. I'll start doing this with Victor next time. I'll also do everything I can to make it a goodbye that Victor can understand and accept," I explain.

Fredrik nods to show he understands, but he is still worried that his son might need more help. We talk about how Victor will continue to work through his loss together with his dad and other adults, even after therapy is over. All children must do so. Fredrik himself wants to come back to see me toward the end of the summer and wonders if that might be possible.

"I'd like to check in with you about how things are going for Victor," he says.

He makes it clear that he would feel a great sense of security if we could set up one or two appointments. We decide that Fredrik will come to see me directly after the summer. He wants to make an appointment here and now, so we do so, and Fredrik immediately enters the date and time of day into his pocket computer.

Fredrik has finished his talks with the nurse at the hospital. He stresses that those talks have been invaluable to him and that without them he would have felt like a feather being buffeted by the wind. As intended, he concentrated on himself and his own

situation when he went to the nurse for help. Now Fredrik is plan-
ning to take Victor on a little trip, together with his maternal grandparents, after therapy is finished. They will be away for a few days.

"Then it won't feel so empty," he says.

Our discussion has gone over time, but Fredrik does not really
want to leave. However, I must finally bring the session to a close.
As he gets out of his chair, Fredrik touches his head, indicating that
he has come down with a headache. He has put his head in his
hands a number of times during the session, perhaps to concentrate
and to relieve his headache. He has made use of every minute with
me to talk about Victor and to assure himself that things are going
in the right direction for his son.

Standing in the doorway, ready to leave, he tells me that he was
nervous about coming for this visit. He could not sleep last night.
Now he takes my hand and thanks me. He is truly impressed with
the way Victor gets so completely involved in his therapy and he is
greatly moved by his son's resolute struggle to get over to the other
side of his grief. The last thing Fredrik says as he starts down the
steps is, "You know, I really see it now, there's an entire science to
understanding children who are so young, like Victor."

"You hit the nail on the head there!" I say.

CHAPTER FOURTEEN

Therapy nears a conclusion

Session thirteen: 23 May

Fun with pee pee and poopy

T oday it is as warm, as in the height of summer. The sun is shining and the sky is blue. Victor is in a talkative mood and we can hear how he chirps for himself and with his dad in the stairway. He looks absolutely adorable, dressed in summery new clothes. He is wearing a bright red baseball cap with the big brim hanging down over one ear. His new blue and white striped T-shirt was clean when he left home, but it has become dirty with sand from his morning play. Victor's hands are also sandy. Indeed, it appears that Fredrik has taken his son right out of the sandbox to bring him here. Victor is eager to report, "Daddy's got a baseball cap, too. It's green or black. It's not on him."

"Oh, I see. So both of you have new summer caps," I comment.

Victor beams with pride over his important new cap and wants to tell me more, "The twinnies have, too. They buyed in the shop."

From what he is telling me so enthusiastically, I understand that the uncles bought four caps in different colours, so that each of the guys got one of his own. Victor is quite displeased that his dad left his cap on the shelf down in the waiting room. Fredrik prepares to leave for the other room, where Jorge is waiting for him as usual. As he stands up, he happens to bump into Victor's cap, causing the brim to slide down. Victor reacts immediately and scolds his father sharply, "Shame on you, daddy. What you think you doing?"

"Oops, I didn't mean to do that. Sorry. Come, let me put it back the right way," says Fredrik.

Victor responds loudly, "Can do 'self."

He fixes the cap so that the brim is at its proper angle. I can see how he has practised putting on the cap with his uncles.

Fredrik knows how important it is for Victor to make sure his daddy is well taken care of by Jorge. He asks Victor to go with him so that he can see for himself that things are the way they usually are. Victor does not respond, so Fredrik says again, "Well, come on, now."

Victor shakes his head a little, looking as if he finds it annoying to be reminded, and answers, "Okay, okay. I coming."

Fredrik looks a bit surprised as Victor dashes into Jorge's room and then out again just as fast. Laughing and running, Victor shouts, "See you soon, baboon!"

He slams the door and bounds into the playroom. He is laughing so much that he makes me laugh as well. There is something different about the vibrations that both father and son are giving off today. Something less strained. Victor allowed himself to have fun for a moment, even in his father's presence.

He starts by fetching the cannons and lining them up in a row. He sees them as tractors and says, "I want to play traffic."

He makes the cannons go "vroom-vroom" and "honk-honk" as he drives them around in the wet sand. His hands get even dirtier than they were before. He has a hard time keeping track of his cap, which slides here and there on his head. He makes it clear that I am not to offer him help with his cap. He can take care of it himself, just as he so sternly told his dad. Victor is lively and wants to get a lot of things done today. He tiptoes into the closet, into Villa Villekulla. Stomping around in there, he says, "I fixing stuff for us in here."

Then he comes out and runs over to the toy cupboard. He picks up a little toilet stool, a stove, and a few other things, doing so on the run, without losing his balance in the least. He says, "I need things inside."

After he has been in the closet a minute or two, he shouts a question to me, "You want pancakes?"

He is offering me pancakes but is not inviting me inside, so I sit there outside the villa and answer, "Yes, please. Let's eat together, you and me."

Victor throws me a pancake that he has made on the little doll stove and he downs one himself. It is no longer as important for Victor to give priority to other people's needs. Without asking whether I am full, he calls from inside the closet, "Don't have time for this. I do something else. I going away now."

"I understand that you have lots you want to do before you go. We must say bye, bye to each other before you go. But we're going to see each other two times before that. We don't have to say good-bye today."

As Victor is now starting to talk about going away, I want to use this as an opportunity to talk about the "going away" from therapy that will be coming soon. However, he wants nothing to do with any discussion of parting. Instead, he lets out a burst of giggling and laughing. He puts his hand through the slit in the doorway and waves to me with the little toilet stool. He calls out from inside, where he cannot be seen, "Pee pee and poopy! Pee pee and poopy!"

He laughs at this subject with all his heart, in the way that only a two-and-a-half-year-old can do. It gives me a sense of joy and relief to see this sound and age-appropriate behaviour on his part, to see him having a good laugh at the same things as other children his age. He goes on with his messing around and says to me, "You go pee pee and poopy in this! Poopy too! Fart out your poopy!"

He surprises himself with his courage to talk this way to me, which makes him laugh even more excitedly. I am not the one to put a lid on this laughing, either, so I laugh with him in his delight. We laugh together. I have looked forward to seeing Victor truly happy, if only for a moment, and to sharing this moment with him. He tells me again and again, in the same laughing way, all that he knows about poopy and pee pee. To get him back to reality I finally say, "You're also going to go pee pee and poopy in the potty when you get bigger. It won't be long now. Maybe it'll even happen this summer."

Victor makes this out to be the most hilarious thing he has ever heard. He laughs till he almost chokes and then he falls in a heap on the floor. He stands up, but falls down again in a new laughing attack. After a while I help him to get himself together, and comment, "It's fun with pee pee and poopy."

"Oh yeees!" Victor shouts.

I gradually help him to stop laughing and I lift him up again so that he is standing firmly on the floor. As I am doing so, I can see something in the look he gives me. He senses that we are not going to be meeting so many more times. I want to start talking about this matter, but find no way to get into it from what he is saying or doing at the moment. When he has calmed down, Victor takes out a few toy houses and puts them in the sand. He makes a distinct point of saying, "Someone lives in all the houses."

He pairs every house with a person, a doll, or an animal. Jorge gets a red house with a black roof, dad gets a white house with three floors and a black roof, I get the church, and the grandmother doll gets a white house with two floors and a red roof. Victor fetches the elephant and puts it with a little church. Then he plays noisily that every one leaves home, but where they go is not clear. In any case they soon want to run back to their houses. I want to know where he lives himself so I ask and he answers, "I live with my daddy, of course. In my daddy's house."

He shows me exactly where he lives, pointing to a small window on the top floor of his father's house. Continuing to be a little rambunctious, he screams delightedly, "I'm the el'fant. Trampety-tramp-tramp."

He dashes around with the elephant, who wants to find the way to its home. The elephant does not want to be away any longer, but it is having a hard time finding its home. The little church that is the elephant's home does not even reach the top of its legs, but this does not concern Victor. He puts the elephant right on top of the little church when it finally finds its home.

"El'fant tired and wants to sleep at home."

All this excitement has also made Victor tired. Children who are approaching the end of their therapy usually bring the theme of somebody or something either going away or not going away into their play. This usually means that they know the end of therapy is near, but not necessarily that they have come to terms with ending it.

Figure 13.   The elephant lives in the little church. When he goes for a walk he has a hard time finding his way back home.
Comment.   Victor, too, has to put a lot of hard work into finding new ways back into life.

Where are they?

Victor comes and sits next to me in my easy chair. He leans against my right arm and rests. After a while, I lead into the subject of our approaching ending by saying, "You've come here to see me many times."

Victor understands exactly what I want to talk about, but he does not want things to come to an end. Victor does not want me to go on talking like this. He wants to do something else, something entirely different, but I try once more.

"We have a little more of our sessions left. Two more times."

Victor is not interested, but I want to make it clear to him what I mean by two more times. I call for his attention and hold up both of my thumbs in the air. I wave them both as a way of showing him concretely how long it is till Erica is over.

As a response to my attempt to bring up our farewell, he picks up the two toy hedgehogs in one hand, mumbling to himself, "Little brother and mummy."

"Are you thinking about them?"

He does not answer with words but gives me a ball of plasticine. He brings out two lorries with empty platforms and puts one hedgehog on each platform. He requests of me, "Make locks. Big locks."

I help him and we make big locks out of lumps of the plasticine. Victor wants us to secure the sides so that the platforms of the lorries are closed. He directs me, "We lock very, very carefully. So they not fall out."

Victor puts great effort into locking the lorry platforms with big balls of plasticine because he wants to make sure the hedgehogs will not fall off. However, he makes the lorries drive around so wildly that the hedgehogs fly off anyway. He picks them up and asks me to make even bigger locks. Then he proceeds to drive around even faster and the hedgehogs fall off again, in spite of the big new locks. I knead locks in larger and larger sizes, but nothing helps. Before long, the locks are as large as the platforms of the lorries, but not even this makes any difference. Victor increases the speed and handles the lorries so roughly that the hedgehogs fly off and land under the desk where he cannot see them any more. He gives me a startled look and asks, "Where are they?"

Figure 14. Victor makes strong locks for his trucks so that nobody will fall out as they speed along.
Comment. Victor wants guarantees that there will never be another car accident.

He does not mean the hedgehogs. We both know that. I take a deep breath for courage and ask him, "Do you mean mummy and little brother?"

Victor answers weakly and miserably, "Yes."

I am so struck by Victor's naked admission of his loss that words fail me. At two-and-a-half years of age, he can bring himself to ask where they are and thus risk getting the answer that he dreads most of all. I feel totally drained. How is it possible to explain to this little child about where half of his family has gone? The only thing that seems right to say at the moment is, "I don't know, Victor."

He sits absolutely still as we continue talking quietly and seriously. It is as if he does not dare to move. We talk about how his dad says that his mum and little brother are together in heaven. He also knows that other people say they are at the cemetery. I sit there for a long time and dread what I am going to have to say to him explicitly and finally I say it.

"They're not coming home."

Victor answers, "I'm hungry."

He hungers after his mother and what she used to give him. I want to hook into this and ask, "What would you like?"

Victor's face brightens as he answers, "Pancakes."

"Do you mean your mum's pancakes?"

"So yummy, yummy. She making pancakes now?"

Again I must do violence to my own feelings in order to tell him what he has to hear. "No, Victor, she's not making pancakes now."

To underscore that this is the way things are, I give him the same answer several times in different versions, but I add also, "I know where you can get pancakes that are almost as good."

He looks at me searchingly, but says nothing.

"From your grandma," I continue.

I tell him that his grandma was the one who taught his mum how to make pancakes. That is why we can be sure that grandma knows how to make them. Victor must be wondering how I know this, because he asks, "You seen my grandma?"

"Well, no, I don't know her, but I've heard loads about her from you and daddy. So I know she wants to make pancakes for you. Her pancakes are almost as good as your mum's."

I stay with this topic for a good while because I want to convey that even "second best" can be good enough, if only you dare to try it. It is also important that his mother's pancakes remain the best in his memory. He is starting to be able to transfer the expectations and wishes that he previously associated with his mother to other persons, among them his grandmother. As times goes on and he does so more and more, it will be easier for people around him to meet his needs. To round off the session, I say, "Let's go and get daddy so you two can go home together, okay?"

Victor is fiddling with his new cap and answers me in a somewhat mischievous tone, "Nooo!"

I come back jokingly, "Yes, let's do it."

"No, let's not."

"Oh, yes, let's go."

"Oh, no, not go."

"Oh, yes, let's go."

This is his way of showing me his ambivalent feelings about ending this session and therapy as a whole. I want to help him over the hump so I say, "Thanks for today, Victor. It's over for today."

Victor starts to bounce around the room, throwing his cap, so I say, "It's hard to say goodbye. For now, let's just say bye, bye for today. Then we'll meet two more times. After that, you and dad will say goodbye to Jorge and me."

Victor keeps on resisting and does not want to go home. Finally, I lift him up on my arm, carry him into Jorge's room and deposit him on his dad's lap.

"Victor doesn't want us to quit today," I explain.

"I don't want to, either," says Fredrik.

"But we have two sessions left," I say.

"Yes, oh yes, I know, I know only too well," Fredrik sighs.

Before they start down the stairs Victor fixes his baseball cap so that the brim is at the back. He looks expectantly for my reaction. I remark that the twins have bought good-looking caps and everyone can wear his cap the way he wants to. Victor's cap suits him well, indeed. Later, as Jorge and I stand there watching the two of them going down the stairs, we both notice that Fredrik's steps are somewhat lighter than earlier.

Jorge and I sit down together to regain our strength after our sessions. Today Fredrik has told Jorge that it means a lot to his family that he has brought Victor to us for therapy. They are all interested in "Erican" and in those of us who work here. Grandmother has told Victor that she would like to accompany him here. She says she also needs to play with the toys in the sand tray. Victor immediately said, sure, she could come to therapy with him, that was okay with him. Fredrik said that it had almost sounded as if Victor was ready to give up his own session for his grandmother. But only almost. Fredrik had been careful to point out that "Erican" is for Victor.

Fredrik is concerned about his parents-in-law and thinks that they also need the kind of help that Victor and he have received. However, the in-laws have said that they do not want to go to a psychiatric clinic. Jorge has told Fredrik that there may be someone at their church whom they could talk to.

Fredrik's mother-in-law feels the loss of her daughter Malin and grandchild profoundly, and sees no end to the suffering she is going through. She cannot sleep at night. When her daughter was alive, she spoke to her on the telephone virtually every day. Malin and her sister Anna also kept in touch through frequent phone calls. Now Anna and her mother call Fredrik the way they used to call Malin. They cannot possibly have the same kind of talks with him that they had with Malin, he says. Fredrik cannot stand speaking on the phone for any length of time. Every time he and his mother-in-law talk they are reminded of their great loss. Fredrik has asked Anna what she and Malin usually talked about during their long phone calls. Anna has not been able to explain this, but she has an enormous sense of loss.

CHAPTER FIFTEEN

Session fourteen: 6 June

I want Erican forever and ever and ever

L ast week I unfortunately had to cancel Victor's session because I was down with a bad cold. Fredrik did not come to see Jorge, either. We decided just to move the schedule forward by one week, so that they would still get their last two sessions. Today they are five minutes late. As they step into the playroom, Fredrik explains that they missed the bus. Victor had a tough time leaving his day-care today when everybody was outside playing and having fun. Both Fredrik and Victor have become more relaxed about getting here on time. Previously, it was absolutely crucial that they not lose a single second of the session.

A soft summer rain is falling outside. Victor is wearing his rubber boots, but his socks have somehow disappeared. His T-shirt is hanging down outside his trousers and he is clutching his cap in his hands. His clothes are not in such perfectly neat order as many times in the past. Again, he looks as if he has come here right out of the sandbox. His hands are sandy in spite of a quick wiping off. Victor has painted his nails with a red magic marker. Everything about him shows that he takes part in the activities at day-care and has fun doing so. He looks content.

Fredrik says goodbye to his son, not expecting Victor to follow him into Jorge's room, and, indeed, he does not. Victor does not call out after Fredrik, but trusts that his dad can manage on his own. He clomps around in the room in his boots, which slip because he does not have any socks on his feet.

He steps right into the closet and wants me to join him.

"Come into Villa Villycoolly," he calls.

I squeeze myself in as much as I can. Since Victor wants to close the door, he says sternly, "Come on, come in here. Not stick out."

He tries to pull me in while he mumbles that my legs are too big. He soon realizes the futility of what he is doing. There is not enough room for me in the closet this time, either. There is an even greater mess, with toys and things spread over the floor. However, I stay with him in Villekulla, even though I am only half-way in, as long as I can. When it gets too uncomfortable for me to go on standing bent under the sloping roof, I suggest that I go out into Pippi's garden. Victor likes my idea and says, "Wait for me out there."

"Okay."

Closing the closet door, he calls out, "Is Mr Nilsson there?"

"Yes, and Little Old Man is too," I answer.

"What they doing?" asks Victor.

I wonder if he is actually referring to his dad and Jorge so I say, "They're in the other room, talking."

Suddenly he says through the closet doorm "Not call me."

"Okay, I won't."

"You help to me?"

"Yes."

Victor occupies himself quite a while in the closet without making a sound. It seems as if he needs time to reflect over something. I leave him alone until he climbs out of the closet. He goes to the sand tray and starts to poke around in the wet sand with a pail and shovel. He thinks this is great fun and gets messy all the way up to his elbows.

Victor wants to make balls out of the wet sand and needs my help to make the desired sizes. A big and a little round ball. He wants them to be the same size as the plasticine balls I previously helped him to roll. He puts the balls in the middle of the dry sand

and wants us to sift sand over them together. He wants us to follow exactly the same procedure as the previous time with the other balls. He makes a recurring comment, sometimes put as a question, and he says it as though he is seeking reassurance. "You help to me?"

Every time he says this, I assure him that I will help him. I ask myself if he needs this reassurance because I had to cancel our session last week. I sense that he has somehow understood that the cancellation was a breach of our original agreement.

"I'm so sorry that I couldn't see you here last week," I say.

He does not answer. We continue to spread sand over the balls. He goes on saying, "You help to me."

"Yes, I'll help you. Show me what you want me to do."

Victor answers by pouring sand in my cupped hands. He wants me to spread more and more sand over the balls and says, "Make them go away. No more see them. More!"

It is clear that we are performing a symbolic act when we bury a big and a little one today, exactly as we have done previously. He is intent and resolute about this work and says finally, "Now enough. Now can't see them. They all gone."

I suggest that we rest a moment. I need to collect my thoughts about how to proceed. I want to agree with him and yet not, so what I decide to say is, "Yes, you're right, Victor. You cannot *see* them but you can *feel* them with your hands."

He is totally still, looking at me with his blue eyes wide open.

"I'll help you. I'll show you how we can do this," I explain.

I want to relay to him that even though you can no longer see certain things or certain people, you can recall them with other senses than sight. This way you can keep them inside you. I take his hand in mine and put it carefully on the sand. We feel the tops of the balls many times. We touch them both softly and forcefully and we pat and stroke them. We sift more sand over the tops of the balls and again we trace their contour with our hands. Victor does not want us to dig out the balls, no, he wants them to stay buried. The atmosphere is charged with meaning. I am filled again, as so many times before, with wonder over this child, so young, so vulnerable, yet able to work through his great loss.

After today there will be only one session left. I want us to talk about ending our work at "Erican". One way to approach the end is to talk about how things were at the beginning. I say that we have met many times and now we will meet only one more time before we have to wave goodbye to each other. Fredrik has told Victor that they are going to take a trip with his grandparents when our sessions are over and Victor is looking forward to this trip.

To bring in the time perspective, I mention the snow and cold when he came the first time. Now the sun is shining and it is warm outside. In the beginning he and his dad walked here, but now they take the bus. I add that I remember that dad was so very sad then and Victor had to help him. Victor was also very sad and did not know what to do. Up until now Victor has listened solemnly, but now he wants to do something else. I therefore hurry to take off the lid of his box, saying, "Come, let's look at all the things in here. We saved them because we thought they were important."

To look one last time at the items in this box is a concrete way of looking back at Victor's work in therapy. Here are the queen in her red cloak, a torn-off elf's cap, the grandmother doll with the little telephone, a big and a little plasticine ball, drawings with strokes and marks of several colours, the repaired car, and some other things. Victor looks down into the box and fiddles with the things while I make comments about them. I ask if he remembers when he made one of the drawings. He answers by going to get a black marker.

Victor wants to mark on the floor around his box. However, I slip a big piece of paper in under his marker and suggest that he can draw on that. I wonder if his wanting to mark up the floor is a test to see if he has to respect the usual limits to the very end of therapy. Victor has never before wanted to write on the floor. He knows that it is against the rules at home and at day-care, as well as here. He makes another couple of attempts at doodling on the floor, but I stop him. It is important that I keep my word when I tell him that he may not draw on the floor. Otherwise, how can Victor trust that I will keep my word when I say that we are not going to have any more sessions after next time?

When it is completely clear to Victor that I am not going to let him doodle on the floor, he stops trying and instead fetches a black pen for me. He says, as he sticks it in my hand, "Draw together."

I ask, "What do you think we should draw?"

There is no answer because Victor gets distracted. He suddenly discovers the socks that are supposed to be on his feet. They are in one of his jeans' pockets. He pulls out one sock at a time and waves them around. Sand whirls out. I want to keep his attention on what we just started and say, "I'll help you put your socks on later. Let's colour first."

Victor is aware that I want to talk about our parting and this makes things hard. With a laugh, he tosses his socks up in the air and they land on my desk. I reach out my hand to him and ask him to come and sit with me on the edge of the sand tray. He takes my hand and wants to sit on my lap. We sit down on the floor and I start to draw with him on my lap. After a few drawings I draw a black cross on the paper. Victor wants to draw a cross just like mine, but his drawing comes out as just a black line.

"Draw lots of those. Draw crosses for me," he pleads.

For every cross that I draw Victor wants to draw one just like it but the lines he draws are crooked and squiggly. He compares our crosses and sees that they do not look the same. He looks unhappy and says sadly, "Oh, no, look. I can't do it. My ones don't look good."

"No, Victor, I know, but that's okay. You're only two and a half years old and no child your age can draw crosses. It's too hard. You'll be able to do it when you get bigger. I'm sure you will."

Suddenly I hear some loud bumping sounds outside our room. It sounds like a child is running past and then down the stairs at breakneck speed. There is a shriek and a howl and a mother's consoling voice. Victor is totally absorbed by his own emotions and notices nothing. I ask him, "Have you seen crosses like these?"

He answers directly by scribbling over two of the crosses. It is no longer clear that they are crosses. After messing up these two crosses, he does not seem to want to mess up any more. I think we need to talk about crosses that he is likely to see in real life.

"I know where there are crosses like these," I start.

Victor sits quietly, leaning against me, letting me speak.

"At the cemetery. There are both big and little crosses at the cemetery," I continue.

Victor does not move. I say that his dad has told me about a big cross on his mother's grave and a little one on Oliver's. My throat tightens and it is hard for me to speak, but I concentrate all my strength into trying to continue, "You don't like to go and see the crosses. I know it makes you feel strange. You don't know how to act when you're there."

Everything is so silent that I feel compelled to make sure he is actually breathing. When I have done so, I go on, "Well, that's okay. No little boy or girl knows how to act when they see crosses. It's hard for grown-ups, too."

Victor knows that it is hard for big and little ones and he answers by saying, "To be near, to be near."

I have heard him say "to be near" on several previous occasions. I can guess that he has heard adults use this expression and that he repeats it without really understanding what it means. Dad and the other grown-ups are the ones who want to go to the cemetery to be near.

"Children usually want to go to the place where the crosses are when they get bigger. Jorge and dad have talked about that," I say, to round things off.

Again, Victor says, "You help to me."

Again, I answer in the affirmative, but he does not seem quite satisfied with my answer. I am wondering if he is actually asking me how *long* I will be helping him. Therefore I say, "I've helped you many times. I'm helping you today and I'll be helping you one more time. After that, we have to say goodbye to each other. Then you will be at home with your dad and at your day-care."

"But I want Erican forever and ever and ever."

"Well, indeed, you've come here to Erican many times. You've liked coming here. I've liked having you here, too. We've both liked our meetings."

Many years of experience as a child psychotherapist have taught me how important it is to put a lot of serious work into preparing for an impending farewell. I know full well that it is often the most difficult part of therapy work, both for the child and for the therapist. If I did not possess this knowledge, it would be even harder to withstand Victor's pleas to continue coming to Erican. It is hard enough as it is.

We console each other

Victor gets up to fetch the sandy socks that landed on my desk. As he stretches to reach them he discovers that my desk is unusually messy, with piles of folders, papers, and books. On top there is a spiral notebook with the notes that I have entered after all of Victor's visits. He is curious, points to it, and asks, "You draw stuff on your paper?"

I fetch the notebook and thumb through it to show him all my writing and I tell him what I have done.

"I've written down what you've played and what we've talked about. I've also made notes about things your dad has told us. By writing things down this way, I've ended up with a diary. What is written here is very important. I read it so that I can remember all these things."

Victor does not understand everything that I am telling him, but he looks interested and continues to turn the pages. I read some excerpts aloud to him, excerpts about the aeroplanes, the queen, the cars, Pippi Longstocking, the big and the little one, the hedgehogs, and other things. While he is turning the pages, I notice that I have accumulated lots of notes indeed. I am struck with the idea that I would like to write a book about Victor's therapy. In that case I would base it on the contents of his box and my notebook. We keep turning the pages until we get to a blank one.

"Let's write about how things have been at Erican," I suggest.

The air in the room feels as though it is pulsating with tension and anticipation. Victor shows that he likes my suggestion by putting his marker down where he wants me to start writing. I draw a little figure and ask, "Who's this?"

"It's Victor."

"Is he happy or sad?"

"Sad, of course."

Victor wants me to draw more figures. I draw another little boy and before I even put in the mouth he says, "There I happy."

I draw a bigger person and he says, "It's dad. He have to be sad."

Victor points at the little boy and says, "There, I make feel daddy better."

The next figure I make is a dad who is happy like the happy boy. Victor points at the happy dad and the sad boy at the same time, and says, "Daddy make me feel better. Draw me on him."

I put a sad boy on the arm of the happy dad. I am deeply moved by what we are doing and feel as sad as Victor does. He notices this and says, "Draw you, too. But you have to be like you were before! I mean haaappy. A happy face. I mean it. Draw a happy Ericabeth. Do it!"

On a new page in the notebook I draw myself with a smile. For Victor it is important that I am happy both on paper and in reality. He is eager for me to continue drawing.

"Draw Jorge and daddy, too."

I do as he wishes and place Jorge and daddy next to the figure that represents me. He goes on with his instructions. "Jorge have a happy mouth. He holds daddy's hand. Daddy crying."

I give Jorge a happy face and I put two tears on daddy's face, but only two. I want to show that he, with time, will be less sad and is going to have fewer tears. Next to dad I draw a happy boy. Now the four of us are there, Victor, dad, Jorge and I, all in a row, holding hands. We look once more at all the people on the page and I say, "Now we've written about how things have been for dad and you during our meetings here."

I am inclined to consider the drawing work finished at this point. I assume that Victor is as exhausted as I am, but he wants to continue.

"Now grandpa and grandma."

I draw his maternal grandfather with a little hair around the edges of a bald crown, and he is holding grandmother's hand. They are both sad, but grandmother most of all, so she gets the most tears. On the remaining blank space on the paper Victor wants me to draw his father's mother and father. Suddenly he lets out a shriek and taps violently on the figure representing Fredrik's mother. "She must be happy. She must, must, must, must, must! I mean it!"

Fredrik's mother is going to come for a visit soon. Victor wants her to be like she was before. He likes her the way she was, not the way she has become. He wants his old grandma back. I draw his paternal grandparents without tears to convey hope for the future and say, "Your grandma is going to get happier. Soon you can do fun things together again. She's going to want that."

"She must," is his curt answer.

As time goes by and his grandmother keeps feeling his longing for her to be her "old self", she will find the strength to do so. She has no choice, because Victor is totally irresistible in his determination.

Both of us are now totally exhausted by the intensity of the session. Victor suddenly decides to quit ten minutes early and I catch him as he starts to dash out of the room. He grabs a can of paintbrushes, but does not know what to do with them. He comes up to the easy chair where I have sat down and places himself squarely in front of me. To get even closer, he wedges himself in between my knees and puts his face right up to mine. He stands still and he has big tears rolling down his cheeks. As more and more tears fall, I am so starkly affected that I cannot say a word. Instead, I do the only thing that comes to my mind.

I take a big, soft paintbrush out of the can that he is still holding in his hands and I stroke his cheeks with it. I want to gather up all his tears in the brush. He is standing absolutely still, with his eyes closed and with tears streaming down his face. I put my arm around his back and continue to brush lightly over his cheeks until the brush is completely drenched. As Victor's tears slowly subside, my own take their turn. Today's session, the next to the last one, has been heart-wrenching and I am so exhausted and moved that my head is spinning. But it is not over. My emotions reach even greater intensity when Victor takes a paintbrush from the can, a brush that some child has used and not cleaned, and starts to brush my face. I close my eyes as he brushes and polishes my cheeks. When I have regained some of my composure, I conclude our session by saying, "We make each other feel better. You and your dad also make each other feel better. It's a very good thing to do."

"Yes, each other."

"Bye now, Victor, thanks for today. We'll have our last session next time."

As I watch Victor leave the room to go fetch his father, it occurs to me that he has not been the least bit wobbly today.

Jorge is also totally exhausted after his talk with Fredrik today. He is just as moved by Fredrik's never-ending struggle as I am by Victor's. Fredrik is trying in every way he can to rebuild what is left of his family. He has changed things around a little at home, but just a little, so as to better accommodate them now that they are two. He says that the state of constant and immeasurable despair that he felt before has started to let up just a little bit. He finds that he can concentrate and think about other things for short periods of time.

He is working more now and goes in to the office every day. This regular schedule does him good. It also makes life more stable for Victor when he spends each and every weekday at day-care. When Victor sees that Fredrik is feeling better, he can be more relaxed and at ease at day-care. Jorge has told Fredrik that children usually have an easier time going on with their own activities and being without their parents when they see that their parents are starting to feel better. Fredrik never ceases to be amazed over how much Victor takes in of what is going on around him.

Fredrik's father has managed to persuade him on several occasions to drive the car that he handed down to him. Fredrik is relieved to find himself capable of driving. He had been convinced that he would never want to drive a car again. He has gained four pounds, but his doctor tells him to gain back all the thirty pounds that he has lost. Fredrik mentioned with a smile today that his father had told him not to wash and scrub Victor so much. Grandfather does not think that excessive washing is good for a child. Fredrik says that he is lucky to have people around him who let him know when he is doing strange things. He includes Jorge and me in this group.

When Fredrik finds Victor deep in thought nowadays and asks him what he is thinking about, he answers, "Mum." Likewise, if Fredrik is asked by Victor what he is thinking about, he answers, "Mum and Oliver". These moments no longer create such a panicked atmosphere as they did earlier. Now they dare to leave each other alone, in peace and quiet, for a while. Fredrik says that he is now confident that Victor will come out of these brooding spells, because he seems to have learned how to do so in therapy.

Another telephone call to the day-care centre. 7 June

Day-care is a free zone

Fredrik is eager for me to call the day-care centre again, so I call Lotta a second time to catch up on how Victor is doing. She is still the one to whom Victor turns first, whether in joy or in sadness. She describes how he has undergone a gradual change. Right after the accident he was wound up and clowned around more or less the whole time. Now, in contrast, he is calmer and more focused, and sometimes he sits absorbed in his own thoughts, as though he is thinking about his mother.

Lotta says that Victor cries easily, over small things, and frequently. Sadness overtakes him when he is tired or hungry or when something does not go his way. Lotta tells me that when Victor slips into his own thoughts, one of the staff members usually sits down next to him. He shows that he does not want to talk, but just be. It is as if he needs these reflective moments from time to time. The teachers leave him alone for a while and then they try to interest him in some activity. If they interrupt him too early, he usually balks and gets cranky or wound up. I get the impression that Victor draws strength from these quiet moments.

Even though it is emotionally demanding for the staff to see Victor so sad, it seems more natural and appropriate, in Lotta's opinion. It was hard to watch him earlier, the way he would do tricks and clown around so that the other children would laugh at him. He seemed to pull them into his state of agitation in some strange way.

Lotta says that the staff have spoken about their reactions with a psychologist who has visited them a couple of times. They all agree that these talks have put them more at ease and have helped them to understand their own reactions better. The staff member whose mother just recently passed away, and who had to take an extended leave of absence, is back at work again.

Overall, things are going well between Victor and the other children. He is well liked and has a lively imagination. Sometimes he breaks in and starts talking when it is another child's turn at circle-talk time. He loses patience when he must wait for the others to try to express themselves. He is told to wait his turn, because the staff have decided to apply the same rules to him as to all the others. However, they all think that this is hard. It is tempting to let him have a little extra leeway and to overlook his missteps. As I listen to Lotta, it is clear to me how fond she is of Victor. She says he is a real personality.

On one occasion when Victor was waiting to be picked up by Fredrik to go to therapy, Lotta mentioned my name. She recalls that Victor had never before frozen her out as he did then. He walked out, with his nose in the air and his cap askew, without even saying goodbye. I give Lotta my interpretation of this. I think that Victor needs to have day-care as a free zone. He does not want to bring in anything that reminds him of the terrible things that have happened. Therefore, he does not want to mix day-care and therapy. Children often react this way.

I comment about the importance of the daily rhythm of day-care for Victor, with circle-time, play, lunch, nap, outside play, and snacks. Lotta agrees, and adds that Victor keeps close track of what they are going to do each day. Also, he always knows on which days Fredrik is going to pick him up for therapy. I ask how the other children and their parents react to Victor and his father. Lotta answers that their reactions have also undergone a gradual change. In the beginning, when the children asked questions about Victor's mother and little brother, it happened that an older girl came to Victor's rescue, chastising them for asking a question that would make Victor feel bad.

Thereafter, the children turned to Fredrik with their questions for a period of time. Lotta thinks it was brave of him to take on these questions. Nowadays the children hardly ever ask about Victor's mother or brother. Lotta adds that just a day or two ago she overheard Victor say "My mum is in heaven" to another child while they were playing with cars. The other child, who is also two years old, had given Victor a wide-eyed stare and then had continued moving his cars around and making car noises.

I ask Lotta about the children's photo albums, since we had talked about the emotionally charged situations that these used to cause. When a new child arrives at day-care with his album, all the other children take out their albums as well. Everyone wants to show his or her parents, siblings, relatives, and pets. Lotta has snapped some recent shots of Fredrik and Victor and added them to the album so that Victor can take pride in showing his "new family".

The day-care centre is a parent-owned cooperative, and Malin used to spend a lot of time there. Many photos from past outings and parties are posted on the walls. Malin appears in a number of these, and sometimes Lotta and Victor look at them together. Lotta says it gives her heart pangs every time she thinks about how Malin is gone forever. She liked Malin so much, as did all of the staff, and they miss her and her enthusiastic involvement in the centre's work.

Lotta makes a point of telling me how much she and the other staff members have appreciated having someone with whom to share the responsibility for Victor's well-being. She is so pleased that he has had a chance to go to crisis therapy. I conclude by saying that I believe Victor and his dad have everything it takes to go on with their life together. They can make it a good life and have a good future.

CHAPTER SIXTEEN

Session fifteen: 13 June

Why we came here?

Victor and Fredrik are right on time today, even though they have had trouble getting here because of traffic delays and jams. Victor looks as if he has just woken up. He has a new, trendy hairstyle that makes him look like a fashion-conscious schoolboy. Fredrik has both of their caps in his hand as they enter the playroom. Victor remains standing in the middle of the room, rubbing his eyes and complaining, "I'm thirsty."

I suggest that we go together and get him a glass of water, but he wants me to go alone. When I return with the water, he does not want it and Fredrik drinks it instead.

As this is our last session, I think it is a good idea for Victor and me to accompany his dad into Jorge's room. I want Victor to see that everything is as it should be, so that he can feel at ease and take full advantage of this last session. Jorge greets father and son as usual and sits down in his easy chair. Victor, who is now wide awake, is keen to go back to the playroom. He scurries off, and after he has closed the door behind us, he says, "We take the blue bus today. The red's better. I mean it, I really do."

I respond matter-of-factly, "Things are different today from how they usually are. You and dad had to take the blue bus instead of the red one. Another thing, this is the last time for you and me to meet. This is the last time for you and dad to take the bus to come here."

Victor protests, "I come here many times. I want to."

We talk about his wish and I say, "Yes, I know. You've liked coming here. You've liked seeing me and I've liked seeing you, too. Daddy has liked talking to Jorge and Jorge has liked talking to daddy. That's the way things have been."

He says, "Then I keep coming."

"Well, actually, what you'll do is keep going to your day-care, just like you usually do."

Victor adds, "And with the twinnies."

I tell him that he is right, that he will keep on doing things with the twins as well. I do not get a chance to say any more, because Victor breaks in, "I got super sad when we wait for the bus. It not come. I cried, and my daddy too. Shame on you, blue bussy!"

I want to use this last session to talk about how hard it is to say goodbye, so I say, "Victor! You know what? I think you two got sad because we have to say goodbye to each other today. Both of you started to think about how hard it is when you don't get to see someone you want to see."

Victor says with conviction, "I want to see you really, really much."

"And I've looked forward to seeing you really, really much when you've come here for your sessions. You've been here many times. Now we'll soon say goodbye. That's hard for both big and little ones."

Victor is listening, so I continue, "It's hard for you and your dad, and for Jorge and me, too. But you two can do it, I know you can."

I turn to the subject of why Victor and his dad came to see us in the first place. I talk about what a long time ago that was. Three months are a long time when you are two and a half years old. I say that I remember their first visit.

"Do you know why you came here?" I ask.

He answers by posing the same question to me, "Why we came here?"

"Your daddy called and told us that your mother and Oliver had died. Jorge and I understood that you two were very sad. Well, we help many boys and their dads, that's why you're here. We wanted you to come in to see us. Your dad thought that would be a good idea, too. Since then we have seen each other many times."

"Yes, I know," Victor says.

He lets me say everything I have to say, and after a short pause he cries softly in a small, miserable voice:

"My mum is dead."

With a huge lump in my throat, I affirm, "Yes, she is."

He sits close to me and watches my mouth as I speak.

"Your little brother, Oliver, is also dead," I continue.

"Yes," he says in a thin voice.

We sit still and talk. After a minute or two, Victor goes to fetch a piece of paper and returns with it, saying, "I draw a happy boy."

Victor wants to feel happy again and puts a great effort into drawing. He makes a little line that has a curlicue for a head at one end. He is content with his drawing and says, "I going to draw you. I make you like you usually are. I draw you haaaappy! You have to be happy!"

On the same paper he draws a longer line with a larger curlicue at one end. When he has finished drawing both himself and me, I ask him if it would be all right for me to give us arms. Victor nods in the affirmative. He shows me where he wants me to start drawing. I draw the arms so that the figures are waving goodbye to each other. All of a sudden Victor says resolutely, "I going to draw on your papers. That I coming back."

He takes my appointment book and puts long lines on many of its pages. He knows that I normally use this book to write down when he and his dad are to come for their sessions. I show him the page where I drew a dad and a little boy the very first time we met. He goes over the drawing lightly with his little index finger. Then I take the book, thank him and say, "I'm going to save what you've written in my book today, the last day. I think that all those lines you've drawn show how much you've liked to come to Erican."

I point to all his lines as I read my thoughts into them, "You've also liked the way dad's had a chance to talk to Jorge. It has helped, Victor, it really has!"

He repeats after me, "It has helped, it really has!"

"It has helped because now you can play again even though you're sad sometimes. You couldn't always do that when you first came to Erican. Sometimes you would forget how to play. Now you remember again."

Bye-bye and thank you

Victor looks around in his box for something important. He lifts out the car that we once repaired with tape and carries it towards me. He wants me to gather all the rest of the cars from the cupboard and take them to the easy chair where he wants us to sit. We load the cars into my sweater, which I stretch out in front of me, and carry them all away. I deposit everything on the floor in front of the chair. He wants us to sit in the same chair and we do so. Then we start to sort the cars and to fiddle with them. Victor recites all he knows about the car makes, but most of his interest is directed toward the repaired car. He says, "It's broken. It's so very much broken. It's very bad on the side."

He points to the part where I have put most of the tape. He points with his little index finger to be sure I look at the right spot and he says:

"It's not broken on the steering wheel. Not broken where daddy sat and drive the car. Most wrecked up where mum and the little baby sat. There, on that side."

I acknowledge that he is right, and he adds:

"I sit behind daddy. It's best."

"Yes, your best place is near your dad. Now it's your dad and you."

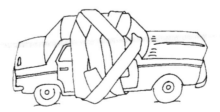

Figure 15.   The car is broken on the side where mum and the baby were sitting. It is not broken on the driver's side.
Comment.   After working through the trauma in symbolic play, Victor finds words of his own to describe reality.

Victor shows that he wants to talk about something else, so I say, "Daddy has told me that you two have been out riding in your new car with grandpa. What's it like to ride in that car?"

"It's okay."

"How do you like the car?"

"Yes, the car. Don't like it."

Cars and car makes are no longer Victor's great interest.

He feels the session coming to an end and he goes up to the sand tray. He puts a camel and a dromedary in the sand and I help him hitch up a little red cart behind each of them. I put a boy doll in one cart and a girl doll in the other. Together we make them wave goodbye to each other. It makes me smile to think that the camel and the dromedary might symbolize Jorge and me.

Victor knows that we are about to say farewell to each other and conclude our sessions. I want us to go and join Fredrik and Jorge so that Victor's dad can be present when we say goodbye. I suggest to Victor that he can wave goodbye to the playroom before we go. He waves, saying, "Bye-bye room. Bye-bye sand. Bye-bye toys."

Putting his little hand in mine, Victor leaves the room with me. The solemnity of the occasion is palpable. I close the playroom door and we go in to be with Fredrik and Jorge. Victor climbs up on his

Figure 16. A camel and a dromedary each pull a doll in a cart. They stop and wave goodbye to each other. Victor says goodbye to Ericabeth, the sand and all the toys.

Comment. After saying goodbye to therapy, life goes on for Victor.

dad's lap. We sit and chat for a little while as a way of bringing our work to a close.

Fredrik reminds Victor that they are going away with grandma and grandpa for a few days. Jorge and I wish them a good time on this short trip as well as a happy summer. We hope the summer will bring lots of ice cream and outings to the beach. Fredrik turns on his mobile phone and talks about wanting to start working full-time. He checks on the date for his appointment with me after the summer. When parting time comes, I take Victor's little hand, shake it, and say, "Bye-bye, thank you and goodbye!"

I tell him that I want to shake hands with his dad as well. Fredrik takes my hand in a firm grip and thanks me for helping them so much. Jorge also shakes hands with Victor and says good-bye to Fredrik. I encourage Victor to take one last look at dad's room. He takes a quick glance, but then remembers that he and his dad are in a hurry. Before they leave the room, Fredrik puts on his cap and so does Victor. He is careful to make his brim have exactly the same angle as Fredrik's. As they start down the steps, Victor tells us that they are going to McDonald's for hamburgers. We wave, all four of us. They call out their goodbyes several times on their way down the stairs. We call back as we remain standing there outside our rooms.

Jorge and I sit down and take a deep breath. We need to gather together all our impressions and experiences. It feels momentous to have said farewell to Fredrik and Victor after everything we have been given a chance to share with them. The thought of saying goodbye to Victor for the last time is not easy but the thought of his future is bright. We look back at how the sessions have changed and developed.

Father and son are now, six months after the accident, well into their painful journey back to life. Jorge and I are pleased to have been able to help them get started on their way. To complete the journey is going to take time and must be allowed to do so. Following father and son in their grieving process has been emotionally demanding for Jorge and me and we are thankful to have had each other's support in this work. What has been extremely rewarding for me in particular is the way in which Victor has let himself accept help, so that he is now back on the right track in his development.

CHAPTER SEVENTEEN

Therapy is over

It has helped, it really has!

The best medicine for a little child in crisis is loving care, and Victor has certainly had plenty of that. From a psychological point of view, Fredrik has borne his son through his grief and is still doing so. People close to Victor have encouraged and respected his psychotherapy. Fredrik has also seen it as a matter of utmost importance to respect Victor's integrity.

Fredrik's and others' respect has been essential because, after the accident, Victor was very quick to accommodate himself to what he perceived as other people's desires and needs. If he had sensed that people around him were sceptical about his therapy, he could not have benefited as much from it as he in fact did. Thus, it was necessary that Fredrik was given time to clarify for himself where he stood with regard to this kind of help. Once Fredrik had accepted it, going to therapy became a natural part of the weekly routine for him and Victor.

After the accident Victor went into high gear. He acted the clown, was hyperactive, and his "happy" manner seemed to intensify every day. The first time we talked to Fredrik, he told us that

Victor had not once asked for his mother or little brother, or for his blankie.

At the time of the accident Victor was in an intensive phase of development. After the disaster he continued to develop new skills as if nothing had happened. He increased in capability, independence, readiness to cooperate and responsibility to a degree that was perplexing. All this made it hard for Fredrik to understand Victor's true psychic condition. His inner state was covered up by these new abilities, which he used in order not to fall apart inside.

The psychological assessment showed that behind his "happy" surface Victor was in a state of shock and chaos. He was filled with overwhelming and contradictory feelings, which were totally incomprehensible for him. Nor could he understand where these feelings were coming from. While trying to fill an inner void with clowning, frenzied activities and chatter, he was very tense, as if guarding against a new threat.

Victor was also bewildered by the great changes in people he knew. He took it as his role to make all of them happy again. Victor became the hub around which the life of his relatives revolved, and by his very being he spread an atmosphere of mixed joy and sorrow around himself. This was highly confounding. It is not strange that his knees buckled and he started to wobble. It finally became hard for him to keep himself upright, both physically and psychically.

Victor's whole way of relating to reality gave an impression of impending collapse. If nobody spoke about his mother, he could maintain his fragile psychic balance. However, it was becoming unsustainable, since a longing for his mother had started to grow inside him, even when nobody spoke about her. He showed in many ways that his psychic suffering was intense.

The healing power of play

It is clear that Victor underwent a psychological healing process throughout his entire therapy. His games and general behaviour changed successively in a positive way. Victor sensed after just a few sessions that therapy was something special and that he could get something he needed from it. The sand tray and most of the toys appealed to him.

Moreover, the therapy room was not "contaminated" by sorrow and despair. In this setting Victor expressed his grief in different ways without having to worry about the reactions of other people. My aim was to meet him in his grief and not to shy away from it. This was the case regardless of whether he expressed his grief through laughter or through tears. Victor, basically a cheerful boy, also needed a chance to express joy, without having to experience confusion in those around him.

My task as a therapist has been to keep the trauma in focus, in the right dose each time. As time moved on, Victor gained a clearer and clearer sense of how much he could manage to process each time. He has, as Fredrik says, taken on reality step by step, in child-size portions.

To begin with, Victor was "happy", and my wish was to get behind this façade in order to meet him at the right emotional level. His superficial joviality has abated, as has his hyperactivity. It is now impossible to make a mistake about whether Victor is happy, sad, angry, or tired, because he shows his feelings clearly. Now he can also sit still for extended periods of time to talk seriously and listen. He is not overwhelmed any more by horrifying fantasies. It is no longer beyond him to understand why he is sad, and when a sense of loss towards his mother comes over him, he shows it.

It is now easier for Fredrik and others to perceive when Victor needs help and comfort. Victor is also able to accept the solace that they offer, and this eases his pain. Victor no longer feels an obligation to be the one to console everyone else. He shows his own needs in a straightforward manner and does not feel compelled to cover them up with boisterousness and laughter. Once again he can assert his own will in the manner that is natural for a two-year-old. During the last sessions of therapy, Victor was also walking without wobbling.

When other children ask about his mother, Victor answers, like his father, that mummy and Oliver are in heaven. Earlier, when he refused to answer, it happened that the other children would leave him right in the middle of playing with him. In the therapy room it has been obvious beyond the shadow of a doubt that the memory of his mother and Oliver has returned to Victor. He has shown this by "bringing them into the room". As time has progressed, it has felt more and more as if his whole family were present, mother, father, Oliver and he himself. Dad and he were there in reality and mum and Oliver in his imagination.

I have come close to the feeling that I actually know Victor's mother. This feeling can be attributed to the intensity with which Victor has conveyed his emotional memories. I have definitely received a strong sense of his mother's positive manner and love for her son. My impression is that Victor unconsciously conveyed these memories to me because he wanted me to share them with him. At the end of therapy he was able to talk about mum and Oliver and to use the word "dead".

Through his sessions with Jorge, Fredrik has received help with his function as a father, even when things have been at their roughest. Fredrik tells us that these sessions have been of vital significance for him, to a degree he had never expected. He has become more and more confident that he will be able to manage as a single parent to Victor. The more Victor has sensed this growing confidence within Fredrik, the more he has been able to let go of his self-delegated responsibility for his dad. His need to check on and protect Fredrik ceased during the course of therapy. A warm sense of trust grew in him and he gradually left his father entirely in Jorge's hands.

The psychological balance between father and son has been restored. Now dad is the head of their new family of two. He is the one who decides and takes responsibility, while Victor is his little son. Both Victor and Fredrik have struggled hard and must continue to do so one day at a time after therapy. Needless to say, it is a highly demanding task to work through a loss as terrible as theirs. Looking back at the therapy process, I can truly see the healing power of play. I hope that in the future Victor will turn out to have been right when he agreed with me, "It has helped, it really has."

CHAPTER EIGHTEEN

Four years later

A school boy

F redrik came to see me at the end of the summer following
Victor's therapy. He had had a month's vacation, but instead
of feeling rested by it, he felt a deep sense of loneliness. Victor
was out of nappies during the day and managing it well. He had
started to snuggle with a teddy bear at bedtime as a sort of replace-
ment for the blankie that he lost in the accident. At this point
Fredrik was worried that he would not have the strength to watch
out for subtle signals that Victor might give about how he was
feeling. He asked for some follow-up sessions and I agreed.

Over a period of three years, Fredrik and I met once every half-
year, six times in all. Victor had his third, fourth and fifth birthdays.
I have followed him indirectly via what Fredrik has told me and I
have formed an idea of how he has developed. My impression is
that he has been as healthy in mind and spirit as could possibly be
expected under the circumstances. His development has picked up
from where it was once disrupted and it has gone steadily forward.

At one point Fredrik wondered if he could bring Victor along so
that I could see him with my own eyes. Of course I would have

enjoyed seeing Victor, but the contact between us had come to a natural end. It would not have been fair to give him hope of resuming therapy since he would surely have liked to do so. I also assured Fredrik that, thanks to his detailed accounts, it was not hard for me to follow how Victor's life with his father was going. At another session, Fredrik mentioned how scary it was to think that he almost did not come to therapy with Victor.

One theme in our talks has been to look at Victor's reactions and behaviour and to identify what is normal for various developmental stages, as opposed to what has been caused by his trauma. The age of defiance, typical for two-year-olds, was interrupted in Victor, only to return with full force a year later. During an intensive period he was stubborn, had to have everything his own way. He had to be right all the time, opposed his father and asserted his will in many ways. Fredrik got my support in seeing this as a delayed age of defiance and not as grief reactions.

We have also gone into the importance of treating Victor as normally as possible. It is easy to spoil a child in Victor's situation, to give him more material things, to be more lax in correcting him and to demand less of him than would normally have been the case. I have made it clear to Fredrik that I am impressed by his gentle but firm way of dealing with his son. He is flexible to a certain point but no further, which gives Victor a sense of security. He knows dad has the last word, just as before the accident.

During these years Victor has spent considerable time with his aunt and her family. He has become quite fond of his cousin, who is one year younger than he. The two grandchildren have taken frequent walks to the cemetery with their grandmother. These are solemn visits during which all three have put one flower each on the grave.

Victor's grandmother has albums with many pictures of Victor's mother Malin and little brother Oliver. They look at these pictures now and then, sometimes at his grandmother's initiative, sometimes at Victor's. At times he has asked her about his mother and she has told him. His grandmother has told him that he reminds her more and more of his mother, both in looks and in personality. Victor has liked hearing this. They have also talked about whom little Oliver might have resembled.

For periods of time Victor has been interested in death, and asked Fredrik many questions. He has been wondering where the skeleton goes, what it means be like someone who is dead, why Jesus died, and why their neighbour killed his dog. Fredrik has always taken care to respond as honestly as possible, even to say that he does not have all the answers. Whenever his day-care friends get baby siblings, the question comes up anew of whether Victor is still a big brother or not.

Around Christmas time, both the first and the second year after the accident, Victor had nightmares. Fredrik described him as being in a state between wakefulness and sleep. Victor was anxious, spoke unintelligibly, and did not know where he was. It seemed as if he was reliving the accident and was filled with chaotic feelings. When he woke up in the mornings, he acted as usual and said that he had slept well. These episodes lasted for a week, both years.

Yes, go ahead and write a book

In a talk with Fredrik three years after the accident, I told him that I wanted to write a book about psychological help for little children in crisis. I said I would like to use material from Victor's therapy and asked how he felt about this. Fredrik was immediately positive and interested, and wanted to know more. I told him that I wanted to describe, step by step, how a little child can be helped to recover after a great loss. When he had listened to everything I had to say, he told me, "Yes, go ahead and write a book."

Fredrik wanted to do what he could to help other children who had suffered similar losses. He was convinced that therapy had contributed substantially to Victor's present well-being. He offered to read the manuscript and share his thoughts and experiences. We decided to think about this further and to take it up again at our next meeting. I suggested that at that time we sign an agreement about the conditions of publication. The most important part of this agreement was that Fredrik would release me from my professional pledge of confidentiality and that he would have a chance to read and approve of the manuscript before it was put into print.

We decided to add a few sessions to the original plan in order to talk about Victor and to discuss the future book. Fredrik read the manuscript several times and gave me his viewpoints. Reading the manuscript was a moving experience for him and gave rise to strong and deep feelings. Our last meeting took place four years after the accident. Victor was then six-and-a-half years old, had left his dear day-care behind and was enjoying being a schoolboy.

When the time had come for Victor and his peer group to start school, the day-care teachers had written a short report to the parents about each child. Fredrik brought the report with him and read the description of his son aloud.

> Victor is a secure, cheerful and friendly six-year-old boy. Other children gladly choose him as a playmate. He can be stubborn about getting his way, but it is easy to reason with him and to get him back on track. Victor has good language skills. He has a large vocabulary and has also picked up quite a few English words. He has taught himself to read. His greatest interests are having fun with his friends, reading, playing soccer, and writing the letters of the alphabet. Victor speaks about his dead mother and brother in a calm and natural way.

CHAPTER NINETEEN

Children and trauma

Little children's grief

Children differ greatly from adults in expressing grief over the death of a loved one. An adult can put his pain into words and be comforted by talking to others. He can speak about his loss, about his fear of facing his new life situation, and about his desperation when looking ahead. The adult can understand intellectually that a loved one has passed away, even if he is unable to accept it emotionally.

A little child who has lost a parent has no words for the tragedy itself, or for his longing to have his parent back again. The child cannot express how he feels or consider what the future may bring. Little children live in the here-and-now and expect everything to remain the same. A little child who has had his parents by his side every day of his life cannot embrace the thought that suddenly one of them will never come home again. Nor can the child comprehend that a new baby sibling, who recently came to the family with such fanfare, is suddenly there no more.

It is impossible for little children to form the thought that a parent has disappeared forever, because fantasy and reality exist simultaneously in their world. In their imagination the dead ones live on as if nothing has happened, and in reality they are gone. The child sees nothing strange or contradictory about this. He must, however, be slowly guided to use his imagination as a way of accepting reality. The child must get help to find bearable forms of expressing his grief; for instance, through play and through fantasizing with symbolic content.

My experience tells me that a little child, together with a secure adult, is able to bear working through something as overwhelming and traumatic as the death of a parent. A prerequisite, however, is that the child finds ways of expression that lead the grieving process forward.

Every child who experiences a death in his family needs to have adults close to him who can give him emotional support, solace, and security. However, all children do not need psychotherapy. Every child who is subjected to trauma tries to get a grip on his situation in the best way possible for him in particular at that particular time. Many children are able to express their grief in ways that are understood by the adults who care about them. They show their despair and confusion and can accept consolation. These children often have an easier time getting the help they need help than do children who cannot show how they feel.

It is not unusual for children to show reactions that are counter to what is expected. By being "happy", active, and all too good at whatever they are doing, they try with all their strength to suppress the tragedy that has struck them. These children often strive to cheer up others who are in despair. They behave in a way that makes it difficult for the people in their presence to give them comfort. In a family hit by tragedy it goes without saying that a little child becomes the life nerve. All care and will to live centre around the child, who may have a hard time taking in all this sorrow-laden attention.

Furthermore, it can be difficult to judge a little child's psychic state if he is in the midst of a developmental spurt at the time of the trauma. The impetus within the child to go forward is so strong that, in spite of the catastrophe, he continues to learn and to exhibit new skills. From the outside it may look as if his development is undisturbed and as if he is not suffering. The child's natural capacity for development overshadows the painful feelings that he bears inside himself and that he does not let show. If the people around him are not aware of this, the child has nobody with whom to share his feelings. People then often believe that the child does not understand what has happened.

Psychological assessment. Why?

When does a little child need psychotherapy? This is not always easy to determine. Every child is unique in his grief, and expressions of grief are as many as there are children. Normal expressions of grief must not be taken as a sign of illness and the child's own healing power should never be underestimated. There is cause for concern if the child does not seem to be going forward in his grieving process, or if his grief is starting to be destructive.

If a child has difficulty showing his grief in adequate ways, a psychological assessment may be in order. Of course, such an assessment cannot provide a totally accurate picture of the child's suffering. It can, however, give a deeper understanding of what is going on inside the child and of how this is related to his behaviour and possible symptoms. As part of the assessment, little children are given a chance to express their thoughts and feelings to the psychologist through play. They make their fantasies known directly or indirectly via dolls or other toys. They make stories with toys in sand, draw, colour, and make things out of plasticine.

Of course, the psychologist also carries on a dialogue with the child whom she is assessing, even though he may not have come very far along in his speech development. However, talking is not the most important part. In dealing with little children, wordless interplay has the greatest significance. It is thus quite possible to carry out psychological assessments and crisis therapies on children who do not yet speak very much. Also, children grasp and comprehend much of the spoken language before they are able to talk themselves.

The child must be met at the developmental level that is relevant for him at the time of the assessment. Because of the trauma, the child's development can deviate from what would be expected. In crisis situations children sometimes regress to an earlier developmental stage and behave as though they were younger. They can also rush ahead, become precocious, and act older. The psychologist tries to see what is behind the child's behaviour in order to understand at what level contact can be made. A trusting relationship must be established so that the child will be willing to show himself for what he is and let his difficulties be known during the assessment.

The psychologist gets to know the child by observing him and playing with him during a couple of sessions. It is important to discern which aspect or aspects of everything that has happened are traumatizing the child most severely. This is necessary in order to understand what the child needs most help to work through.

If the trauma goes back to a violent traffic accident, it will have involved several experiences of great intensity and pain. In addition to the loss of human life and its consequences, the conscious survivor will have memories of the moment of collision as well as of waiting for help to arrive. To be one of those who survived can also be hard. However, little children generally do not think in such terms. When they get older, they may need to work through this aspect of the trauma. It can also be extremely frightening for a young child to see how people familiar to him go into despair and change after an accident.

When the psychologist has formed an idea of the child's psychic state, she shares her findings with the parent. Usually, the understanding of why the child reacts as he does becomes greater at this point. For a parent, who is himself in a crisis situation, this enhanced insight can improve the chances of helping the child.

If a child has had another traumatic experience previous to the new one, his reactions to the new one will be significantly affected by it. Regardless of whether the child showed strong reactions on the earlier occasion, what he felt inside can be actualized by the new trauma. In such a case it can be hard to know where the reactions now being observed originate. A thorough description of the child's life before and after the trauma is therefore an essential part of the assessment. The observations made of the child must be understood against the background of his specific life story.

The results of the assessment can lead to the conclusion that crisis therapy is the best way to help the child. This can be the case when a child seems caught up in a pattern of inadequate behaviour or has taken on an impossible role in his crisis-stricken family. It can be hard for the adults around the child to help him change such a pattern or to help him find other ways of dealing with his new reality. In such cases, crisis therapy for the child and supporting sessions for the parent can be of great help. Another approach is to offer supporting sessions only to the parent. The aim is then to help the parent so that he himself can help his child.

As part of the assessment, it is important to gain an idea of what the child's daily life looks like after the trauma. To be able to offer crisis therapy, the psychologist must be assured that the child's social situation is sufficiently in order, with food, rest, warmth, a regular day and night rhythm, and well-established daily activities. The child must be able to come to all of the sessions as agreed and complete the entire therapy. If these conditions cannot be met, the first priority for the child and his family must be to arrange help with practical matters so that they can get a firm grip on their daily life.

Crisis therapy should not be started unless someone can commit to bringing the child to every session. It may be possible for the child to come to therapy later, when his daily life has become more stable. A child can never be expected to process his inner life in therapy if his outer life is not orderly and secure enough. If sessions with the therapist are started and then must end unexpectedly and abruptly, another trauma is added to the one that brought the child to therapy in the first place. It can be yet another incomprehensible separation for the child, which can increase his sense of abandonment and damage his chances of building up a new trust in life.

When a child is in crisis, it always means that those close to him are also in crisis. When a psychological assessment is made on a child, the psychologist must therefore find out how the rest of the family is doing and how much help they are getting.

Crisis therapy

Psychotherapy is a method of treatment for both children and adults who suffer from some form of psychic difficulties. Such a treatment can be undertaken in many different ways and for different lengths of time, depending on the person's problems and the goal of the treatment. If someone wants to change parts of his personality on a deeper level, a longer span of psychoanalytic therapy can be necessary. The time frame for therapy must be seen in relation to the time it has taken for the patient to develop the personality patterns that he needs professional help to change.

In contrast, crisis therapy can provide great help for people who are in a crisis because of a personal catastrophe. Such therapy can be set up in different ways. It can last as long as the need remains or it can be time-limited from the start. Whatever the length of the therapy, the focus is on the trauma that caused the crisis and the reactions that have ensued. A severe personal loss is often what gives rise to the need for crisis therapy. For children it can be the death of a family member or the parents' divorce, perhaps with a changed life situation as a result.

In this book the kind of crisis therapy that is time-limited from the start is described. Such therapy usually takes between twelve and twenty sessions. Crisis therapy is a specific method of treatment and is not to be viewed as a shortened version of a longer, working-through type of therapy or compared to "seeing" a psychologist a few times.

Children who receive therapy after the death of a parent not only form an attachment to the therapist and the free zone that the therapy offers, but also appreciate the help that their remaining parent is getting. It is valuable for the parent to get support for his parenting task in the changed family situation via his own sessions. To be a single parent to a child after becoming a widow or widower is quite different from sharing the parenting with a mate. The talks with the parent should take place at the same time as the child's therapy and should be carried out by a person who collaborates with the child's therapist. This set-up can be recommended even when the parent himself is in crisis therapy if the focus there is on his own grief over having lost his spouse and not on his role as a parent.

Children are loyal. They are quick to take on the responsibility for a parent who is not able to function normally. This burden of responsibility can make it hard for them to take care of their own needs. Many years as a psychotherapist have taught me that children who get their own psychological help are always grateful that their parents are also getting help. This holds true for children of all ages and regardless of the nature of their problems. Only when they see that their parents are getting help can they feel unburdened enough to start concentrating on their own needs. In a similar fashion relatives close to the child always feel relieved when the child starts crisis therapy. Even if they never meet the child's therapist, they feel a sharing of the responsibility for the child's well-being and can thus put more into processing their own grief.

A close collaboration between the child's therapist and the parent's therapist is essential. They must keep each other informed about their respective therapy sessions. The child's therapist provides updates on the course of the healing process in the child. The parent's therapist can then share these accounts with the parent. In turn, the child's therapist needs to know how the child's life is going outside of therapy, and obtains such information from the parent's therapist.

The talks between the parent and his therapist, the sessions for the child together with his therapist, and the collaboration between the two therapists make it possible to identify and to emphasize the strong points that can keep the family going. It is important for both child and parent to find links between their former life and the drastically changed life situation as it is now. Little children need to take in as much as possible of whatever continuity does remain. For example, they always appreciate it when people who knew and liked them before the trauma show that they continue to do so.

In time-limited crisis therapy the number of sessions is decided from the start. It is a method of treatment based on a plan of its own, with a distinct structure and clear focus. The goal is to process experiences and reactions related to the trauma that has caused the crisis condition. If the child wants to deal with things not connected to the trauma, the therapist naturally accepts this diversion for a while. The child must in no way feel rejected. However, the therapist never loses sight of the goal and brings the child back to the focus of the treatment.

The purpose of crisis therapy is to ease the child's psychic suffering. Through therapy, the child gets help in taking the first steps in his adjustment to his changed life situation. The therapist helps the child to find new ways to master his overwhelming feelings. If the child works through such feelings in therapy, his continued development will hopefully not be disturbed by unhealed after-effects of the trauma.

The posture of the therapist towards the child can be described as both active and passive. It is more active than in longer and deeper working-through therapies for children. There the therapist takes a more wait-and-watch attitude, and lets the child be one step ahead. In crisis therapy, the therapist takes a passive posture in the sense that she starts out by watching and waiting, keenly alert to the child's needs. The therapist is open for contact and waits for the child to show that he also wants to interact with her. The child is encouraged to select his own play material, and the therapist subsequently lets all work proceed from this.

The therapeutic posture is active in the way that the therapist is responsible for maintaining the focus that has been defined for the treatment. She must stick to this course even though it can be extremely painful for both the child and herself. Indeed, what can be harder than helping a little child grasp that his mother is dead? The child must both be followed and at the same time gently led through the grieving process.

The therapist must also be active enough to make sure that the processing of difficult feelings happens in just the right doses. This means that she must sometimes hold the child back and sometimes lead him forward. She must stop the child at times, if she fears that a certain theme can become too painful, and then return later to that theme. The child cannot work through anything if he is overwhelmed by his own frightening feelings or impulses. Sometimes the therapist must do the reverse, coaxing the child to approach a certain subject and encouraging him to stay with it for a while. Not to do this in appropriate proportion can contribute to the child's denial of reality.

The therapist must be sensitive to the child's choice of rhythm and pace in his work. It is necessary to establish a secure rhythm during the sessions since the rhythm in the child's own existence has been so brutally broken. If the pace becomes too fast, the child loses control and becomes stricken with anxiety. If the therapy sessions seem too unstructured and slow, the child will not understand what the focus is meant to be. He then does not see the point of the whole thing, becomes uneasy, and changes activities repeatedly without sticking to any one play theme.

If the balance between working through and easy playing is faulty, it is impossible for the child to find new ways of dealing with his reactions and feelings. It also makes the therapist's work more difficult. She has a definite time frame to follow, since it has been decided when therapy is going to end. The therapist thus maintains a high level of awareness as she works with the child during a set number of sessions. She works towards a conclusion that has a specific date.

The therapist must come to an early understanding of what working pace is suitable for the child. The pace must not be too slow, but not too fast, either. It is also important that the child is allowed to express himself in play on a symbolic level, as long as he needs to do so, before the traumatic event is put into words. It takes time, often all the way till the end of therapy, before the therapist and the child can talk about the one or the ones who have died, and use the word "dead".

The methodology of crisis therapy

The working-through process in time-limited therapy is divided into three phases: the initial phase, the middle phase, and the concluding phase. Certain typical themes always come up in the different phases. In order for the treatment to be successful, the child must get help to go through each phase. The phases flow into each other and it is not possible to say exactly when the one ends and the next begins.

Initial phase. The therapist changes her posture through the different phases. Initially, it is mainly a matter of being psychically present with the child. The therapist adopts a receptive and accepting attitude. She listens more than she speaks herself and she observes how the child presents himself and his trauma through play and small talk. The child should feel free to speak and react as he wishes, so the therapist should not say too much too early. The therapist, though she means well, must not be pushy in consoling the child. If she does so, she risks making the child feel that he and his pain are not being taken seriously. There he is with his difficult feelings, and these should not be fended off.

The therapist must let the child understand from the beginning that it is all right for him to show any feelings whatsoever in therapy. It is not unusual for children to feel that they are reacting wrongly in their sorrow. In therapy there is no right or wrong when it comes to feelings and reactions. A child may cry or refrain from crying, laugh, be angry, or despairing. The child may choose freely how to express these feelings, the only limitation being that nothing is allowed to be broken. Neither the child, the therapist, the play material or the room is allowed to be harmed. It is the responsibility of the therapist to make this clear at an early stage, since it gives stability and security to the therapy.

The initial phase usually lasts through the first two to four sessions of a crisis therapy that has been set up to include fifteen sessions. If the child has already gone through an assessment by the same therapist, this first phase can be kept somewhat shorter than otherwise. In such cases the therapist and the child have already had a chance to establish contact with each other. During the first phase the child must come to know, or at least get a sense of, the focus of the therapy. This can be conveyed either symbolically in play or by talking about what has happened and its consequences for the child. How explicit the therapist can be depends on the age of the child.

When the child is as young as two, it can be hard to get across to him in words what he is about to get help with and how many sessions there will be. His sense of time is not such that he can understand information about the number of sessions in the same way as an older child would. Even so, an attempt at an explanation must be made and any available means may be used. My experience tells me that even very young children understand more than we imagine about time limits and about their own needs for help. When it is clear from the beginning how long the therapy will last, both the therapist and the child are likely to be more goal-orientated.

The most essential task during the initial phase is to create a basis for a good working alliance. The therapist's efforts to do so contribute to the child's discovery of therapy as something unique, something he has not previously experienced, and this arouses his interest. The therapist, by being receptive and curious about what the child presents, awakens the child's receptivity and curiosity about what the therapist may have to offer.

Initially the child needs to be reassured that whatever he has been doing to cope with his difficult situation has been the best possible, no matter how he has been behaving. However, early in therapy, the therapist must inspire hope that there are other, less painful, ways to go. The whole family must be convinced at an early stage that they are going to get help to ease their pain.

Middle phase. In the beginning of the middle phase the child has usually reached a point at which he comes to every session with a sense of urgency. Even little children usually try to keep track of which days they go to their therapy. By this time, a good relationship and a good sense of cooperation should be established between the child and the therapist. Parents are often bewildered, in a positive way, by their children's enthusiasm for the therapy sessions. However, they seldom get any coherent answers when they ask the child about therapy. It is hard to put words to the working-through process and, furthermore, even little children experience therapy as something private that they want to keep to themselves. It is thus important to make sure that the child feels it is quite all right for him to keep his therapy to himself. No one should feel rejected or hurt because he does so.

As time goes by, the therapist must take on a somewhat more active posture. As therapy enters the middle phase, she still lets the child take the lead, but she must also begin to guide him towards the themes that have to do with the trauma. Only in this way can the working-through process move along. The harder it is for the child to approach his painful reality, the more active the therapist must be. She has to use all her imagination and empathy to help the child, through play, to approach what has happened. She can only succeed through play that the child accepts and wants to return to. In this play, by using dolls and toys, the child can give expression to feelings and experiences that stem from the trauma. Initially, the child does not need to put himself or his own reality into what he is doing. It is important that the working-through process starts out on a symbolic level.

During the middle phase the therapist provides a secure base in the life of the child. He appreciates the firm and protective framework of therapy. In this atmosphere the child usually starts trying out different ways of expression by changing his play themes or bringing in new ones. The younger the child, the more concrete will be his play as he tries to take in the experiences around the trauma. The therapist lets the child know that what he is doing is important.

To save what the child makes and to remember what he does have great symbolic value. Everything the child produces and other important items are saved in a private box until the end of the therapy.

A little child works through his grief for the amount of time he can cope with it, not longer. He cannot cope with approaching difficult themes for too long a period of time, nor can he play calmly too long. It is therefore absolutely necessary to alternate painful work and easy play during the sessions. Once the child has come into this rhythm, he himself will often sense when it is time to change theme and will need less and less help to regulate the changes. There are a number of changes of play theme during each session.

My experience is that when children have come this far in therapy, they know what they need help with and they know that they are getting that help from the therapist. This holds true even when there is not particularly much talking during the sessions. Children notice that it helps to play. They feel it in their bodies and they work hard as they play to get through the crisis and feel better. Children want to feel well.

Final phase. This period is often composed of the last three to four sessions. For both the therapist and the child, this is commonly the most difficult part of the therapy. The work must lead to a parting according to the original agreement. The time limit is an important instrument in crisis therapy. The therapist must clearly repeat the date of the last visit for both child and parent. The child may want to continue to come, and thus does not acknowledge the end date. It may then be tempting for the therapist to change what has been decided about the end.

The child must, however, be able to trust the word of the therapist without exception. If the agreement is broken and the number of sessions is extended, the child can get the feeling that his therapist does not understand the terror and panic he feels when faced with parting. With this set time frame in mind the central themes of the final phase must be those that deal with separation and final goodbyes. To work through such themes is absolutely necessary for children who have experienced great losses.

In one way or another, all children brace themselves against finishing their therapy. During the last part of the middle phase and the first part of the final phase, the child often starts to hesitate about continuing his sessions, at least according to the conditions set by the therapist. The child arrives late, says that he is going to end earlier or is not going to come any more. He says that he does not care what the therapist thinks.

The therapist has to be prepared for the contrariness that occurs during this phase of the work. A parent's anxiety about the end of therapy can be a contributing factor in this regard. The child's contrariness can take the form of a return to some of the symptoms or ways of dealing with the trauma that he has actually left behind. Such behaviour is typical for the later sessions and does not mean that the treatment has been unsuccessful. My experience is, instead, that the child latches on to this opportunity to work through, for the last time, his separation anxiety.

A child needs to know why his therapy is ending. Besides reminding him that the date of the last session was part of the original agreement, the therapist can point out that the child is now able to play again. Children of all ages understand this reason. The therapist and the child talk about how it was in the beginning, when the child first came to therapy. Back then, he did not feel at all like playing.

As therapy draws to a close, the therapist leads the child back through the different phases. The purpose is to show him that he has worked towards a change. Either the therapist or the child takes the initiative to take a good look at the objects and work that are in his box. They talk concretely about these items and what they have meant during the different phases. Based on this dialogue, the child can also be shown that the work has led him to feel better, even if sadness still comes over him at times. During this phase the therapist tries to approach the child's loss as it appears in real life. For a little child to be able to put his loss into words and to use the word "dead" often takes until shortly before the end of therapy.

When therapy is almost at an end, the child often takes on the traumatic event with a new approach, perhaps in the form of a new play theme. When this happens, the therapist can have good expectations that the child will continue to work with his trauma after therapy. The child's inner work is not over when crisis therapy ends. It must continue together with someone else outside of the therapy. As the child grows, develops, and understands more, new questions regarding his dead parent will arise. The child needs someone close to him who is prepared to share these feelings and thoughts.

A therapist must never become too important for the child. It is a hard, but an essential, balancing act, to offer a child the right degree of contact. It must be brought up clearly and regularly during the entire therapy process that the therapist and the child are working together for a limited time only. If the attachment to the therapist becomes too strong, it may not be possible to phase it out during the final phase. If this should happen, the child would once again feel abandoned when it is time to say goodbye. Thus, the consequences of the trauma would be reinforced.

An end goal for a therapist is that she will not be needed by the child after the therapy has come to an end. She has to trust that the experiences the child takes with him from therapy will carry him through when hard times come. It is to be hoped that crisis therapy can function as a bridge to a new future and contribute to turning an open wound into a healed scar.

CHAPTER TWENTY

The psychotherapist

Working with children who have suffered losses as severe as Victor's is a task of great magnitude and strong emotions. The psychotherapist is in her professional role, but she is also a fellow human being who feels an intense empathy with the child and everyone around him. In therapy she shares the pain and the grief with the child, while at the same time she must not let herself become overwhelmed by the family's tragedy. If she becomes too closely and deeply involved, the potential space that is necessary between the child and herself will be lost. The therapist thus becomes unable to provide professional help, since it is within this space that she needs to work to find new avenues of possibility for the child.

Good self-knowledge is essential for the therapist. She has to be able to sharply differentiate her own feelings and reactions from those of the child. It is especially important not to falter in this differentiation when therapy work gives rise to strong feelings. There is otherwise a risk that she will project her own feelings into therapy, in the belief that they belong to the child.

To be able to offer a child the specific relationship that is necessary for crisis therapy, the therapist must have a high level of competence, and be secure and courageous. In this relationship the therapist must make a conscious effort to let the child have both closeness and distance. This purposely held posture gives the child a needed frame for working through his grief. To achieve this posture the therapist must have solid knowledge of child psychology.

The therapist must be familiar with children's psychic development and also have experience of how children of different ages react to major losses. With this knowledge as a basis, she uses her thoughts and feelings as essential tools in the actual work with the child. Theoretical knowledge and professional consultation, when needed, are the therapist's best safeguards against over-identification with a stricken little patient.

Based on knowledge of how crisis reactions usually evolve, the therapist can give the child hope for the future. She can give the child a sense of stability by making links between his life before and after the trauma. The therapist must help the child to look back at how things were in the past so that he can look forward later on. Thus, the therapist must dare to talk about how life was for the child earlier, when he had his lost parent, and now, when he does not.

A child's psychotherapist soon becomes a very important person, not only for the child but for the whole family. She must react in a sound way when a small child who has lost his mother starts to look for another adult to give him the care that his mother had previously given him. It is not hard to understand that the child may turn to the therapist, of whom he has become fond, when he feels a need to be cuddled.

In such situations it is important to make a family member aware of the child's need for a concrete showing of affection. After that, the therapist can help the child to turn to this person to get his needs satisfied. These situations call for the therapist's awareness of her own reactions. She might fear that she could further traumatize an already traumatized child by refusing some of his needs. However, the therapist must never let herself become overly important to the child.

When someone in a young family dies, people from several generations are stricken with grief. This means that therapists of all ages can understandably identify with someone in the child's family. In order to keep the relationship on a professional level and to counteract over-identification, the therapist must be psychically stable. She must not be in a difficult personal situation herself at the time because, if she is, her own anxiety about coming into a crisis can more easily be brought to the surface. Working through a crisis with a child can then be too much for her. Before a therapist takes on children and parents in crisis treatment after a tragic event, it is necessary for her to make a realistic evaluation of the possibility of her carrying out such a therapy. The therapist must have confidence in her own psychic strength, have enough time to allot, and be assured of support from her institution.

A crisis therapist must have arrived at a personal view towards death. If she is secure in her own position, whatever it may be, this conveys a sense of security to the child. If the therapist has worked through the loss of a loved one herself, this will also be of help in the work. In such a case, the therapist will know first-hand what it is like to regain the will to live and will be able to communicate this to the child. The psychotherapist must be given the chance to work through, with another professional, the feelings and reactions that arise in work with families in crisis.

Psychotherapists who work with small children who have lost a parent are often plagued by a sense of insufficiency. Everything they do can at times seem banal and trivial. Even though it is unrealistic, they cannot avoid being struck at times by an urgent desire to undo the tragic event. Such feelings, as well as anxiety, stress, and exhaustion, which are an inevitable part of this work, call for considerable psychic stamina.

It is important that therapists get support and assistance to safeguard their own psychic well-being and thereby their professional efficiency. Institutions that offer psychotherapy must provide such support to their staff. This can take the form of supervision or consultations with a psychotherapist from outside the institution with solid experience of working with children and adults in crisis. Colleagues can also provide good support in dialogues and discussions, provided that the climate is sufficiently open and trusting.

I see it as essential that two therapists always work together with a family in crisis. Both participate at the same time in the family's grieving process and are thus able to share experiences. They can support each other by a mutual exchange of feelings and reflections. Preferably, there should be an opportunity to do so in close proximity to each therapy session.

To meet with a small child in deep despair and get a chance to follow him through his grief is a gripping experience. The therapist will find it emotionally demanding indeed, but also extremely satisfying, when she succeeds in helping the child to find his joy in life again. If a psychotherapist is successful with her work in crisis therapy, the child will be spared a future of sending out "feel sorry for me" signals to everyone around him. Consequently, the child will not be an object of pity, but will be recognized in terms of his personal characteristics, skills and accomplishments, just like other boys and girls.

CHAPTER TWENTY-ONE

Reflections

Within the approximately six months I spent writing this book about a little child's journey through his grief, two events occurred that gave me extra cause for reflection. From my point of view, as a child psychologist, both events concern children and trauma. One shook the whole world, and the other was of particular significance for Sweden.

I had just started to write when terrorists attacked the World Trade Centre in New York on 11 September 2001. In addition to all the other thoughts that have filled my mind, I have thought much about the some thousand children who suddenly lost one of their parents or another person close to them. Children in overwhelming numbers were struck by a trauma beyond comprehension, and they were badly in need of help in order to go on with their lives.

Infinitely much has been reported in the media about the terrorist attack and its consequences. I have noticed, however, that very little has been written or said about the children who were affected. In contrast, many commentaries have been focused on the adult men and women who lost their partners. Perhaps this indicates that people generally do not regard children's grief with the same seriousness as they do that of adults. Or is it too hard to face children's grief? Whatever the case, we need to rethink our reactions and make sure that children are not forgotten. It is important to be alert to how each unique child expresses his or her grief over a lost parent.

On 28 January 2002, as I was finishing the book, the Swedish author Astrid Lindgren passed away at the age of ninety-four. She has, like no other writer, been of help to children, generation after generation, who have found themselves in difficult situations. Astrid Lindgren stayed young at heart and she certainly knew what she was doing when she created all her stories on the basis of this spirit. Her characters in their imaginary world seem so real and so alive. They become good friends and companions to all the children who meet them in her books.

No situation is too difficult to master for the children who are Astrid Lindgren's main characters. They can stay on top of everything, come rain, come storm. These life-affirming characters inspire hope and have a healing effect on children who are trying to deal with painful aspects of their lives. I have met children who, after a death in the family, have turned especially to Pippi Longstocking and the lovable, indomitable prankster Emil. To work through a trauma, children must have access to different "tools", and Astrid Lindgren's stories provide excellent ones.

For long periods in our lives, we do not give especially much thought to death. When it suddenly strikes among young people, who are right in the middle of their lives, it comes as a shock. It is particularly devastating when a young parent dies and leaves behind small children.

Many adults feel unsure of themselves when it comes to helping children in grief. They see how troubled and hurt the children are and they are afraid of making the pain worse. Some children thus need help from a therapist through crisis therapy. If a trauma is not worked through, its after-effects will follow the child into adulthood and can have disastrous consequences in connection with other life crises. Based on this knowledge, it should always be a matter of course to offer psychotherapeutic help to a family in acute crisis due to a trauma. Decision-makers in society should realize that crisis therapy gives people a chance to have a significantly greater quality of life, at a relatively low cost, and is thus of benefit in a broader societal and economical context.

I have chosen to call the boy in the book Victor, "the conqueror". Through the years I have met many young conquerors who, after psychotherapy, have regained their joy of living and have gone on with their lives.

BIBLIOGRAPHY

Reading for general interests

Axline, V. (1990). *Dibs in Search of Self. Personality Development in Play Therapy.* Harmondsworth: Penguin.

Bendt, I. (1993). *Mörker och ljus. Små barns livsfrågor är också vuxnas.* Stockholm: Verbum Förlag.

Bergman, O., & Normelli, A. (2000). *Den lilla sorgen. En bok om missfall.* Stockholm: Wahlström & Widstrand.

Björklund, L., & Eriksson, B. (2000). *Barnet i mötet med livets mörka sidor.* Stockholm: Verbum Förlag.

Buten, H. (2001). *When I Was Five I Killed Myself.* Edinburgh: Canongate.

Cleve, E. (2000). *Från kaos till sammanhang. Psykoterapi med en pojke som har diagnosen ADHD.* Stockholm: Wahlström & Widstrand.

Cleve, E. (2004). *From Chaos to Coherence. Psychotherapy with a Little Boy with ADHD.* London: Karnac.

Dyregrov, A. (1992). *Barn i sorg.* Lund: Studentlitteratur.

Dyregrov, A. (1995). *Att ta avsked: ritualer som hjälper barnet genom sorgen.* Stockholm: Rädda Barnen.

Dyregrov, A. (1997). *Barn och trauma.* Lund: Studentlitteratur.

Dyregrov, A. (1999). *Små barns sorg.* Stockholm: Rädda Barnen.

Dyregrov, A., & Hordvik, E. (2000). *Barns sorg*. Stockholm: Rädda Barnen.

Edenhammar, K., & Wahlund, C. (2000). *Utan lek ingen utveckling — metoder och förutsättningar för barns lek*. Stockholm: Rädda Barnen.

Eliacheff, C. (1994). *På kroppen och på skriket*. Stockholm: Wahlström & Widstrand.

Falk, K., & Lönnroth, A. (1999). *Nära döden — nära livet. En bok om mod och livsvilja*. Stockholm: Wahlström & Widstrand.

Frédéric, H., & Malinsky, M. (1981). *Martin*. London: Routledge & Kegan Paul.

Gyllenswärd, G. (1997). *Stöd för barn i sorg*. Stockholm: Rädda Barnen.

Gyllenswärd, G. (1999). *Sorg finns*. Stockholm: Rädda Barnen.

Haddon, M. (2004). *The Curious Incident of the Dog in the Night-time*. London: Definition.

Hayden, T. (1980). *One Child*. New York: Avon.

Hayden, T. (1981). *Somebody Else's Kids*. New York: Avon.

Hayden, T. (1983). *Murphy's Boy*. New York: Avon.

Hayden, T. (1984). *The Sunflower Forest*. New York: Avon.

Hayden, T. (1988). *Just Another Kid*. New York: Avon.

Hayden, T. (1991). *Ghost Girl*. New York: Avon.

Hayden, T. (1995). *The Tiger's Child*. New York: Avon.

Hayden, T. (1999). *The Mechanical Cat*. New York: Avon.

Hayden, T. (2002). *Beautiful Child*. New York: Avon.

Hayden, T. (2004). *Twilight Children*. New York: Avon.

Johansson, B., & Larsson, G.-B. (1976). *Barns tankar om döden*. Stockholm: Natur & Kultur.

Kaplan, L. J. (1997.) *Inga röster tystnar helt. När ett barn har mist en förälder, när en förälder har förlorat ett barn*. Stockholm: Natur & Kultur.

Kaplan, L. J. (1995). *No Voice Is Ever Wholly Lost*. New York: Simon & Schuster.

Kide, P. (1991). *En gång ska vi alla dö — en bok till barn och föräldrar om döende, död och sorg*. LIC Förlag.

Larsson, L. (1993). *Törnehäcken. Barn ritar och berättar sig ur kriser och konflikter*. Stockholm: Rädda Barnen.

Lieberman, A. (2001). *Små barns liv. Den känslomässiga utvecklingen mellan ett och fyra år*. Stockholm: Natur & Kultur och Rädda Barnen.

Luterkort, B. (1999). *Barn i bildterapi. Att berätta om det svåra i bilder och videosagor*. Stockholm: Prisma.

Piontelli, A. (1992). *From Foetus to Child. An Observational and Psychoanalytic Study*. London: Tavistock/Routledge.

Raundalen, M. (2000). *Satsa för livet - när barn behöver hjälp.* Täby: Sama förlag.

Stackelberg, E. (2001). *Berättelse för levande.* Stockholm: Journal.

Stern, D. N. (1991). *Diary of a Baby.* London: Fontana.

Ude-Pestel, A. (1985). *Betty. Protokoll einer Kinderpsychotherapie.* Hamburg: Deutscher Taschenbuch.

Reading for special interests

Alvarez, A. (1992). *Live Company. Psychoanalytic Psychotherapy with Autistic, Borderline, Deprived and Abused Children.* London: Tavistock/Routledge.

Alvarez, A. (1998). Failures to link: attacks or defects? Some questions concerning the thinkability of Oedipal and pre-Oedipal thoughts. *Journal of Child Psychotherapy,* 24(2).

Axline, V. (1989). *Play Therapy.* Edinburgh: Churchill Livingstone.

Boalt Boëthius, S., & Kihlbom, M. (Eds.) (1998). Åtta uppsatser om barnpsykoterapi. Ericastiftelsen. Rapport nr 10.

Carlberg, G. (1994). Dynamisk utvecklingspsykologi. Ny utökad och omarbetad utgåva. Stockholm: Natur & Kultur.

Carlberg, G. (1997). Laughter opens the door. *Journal of Child Psychotherapy,* 23: 331–349.

Carlberg, G. (1999). Vändpunkter i barnpsykoterapi. Psykoterapeuters erfarenheter av förändringsprocesser. Akademisk avhandling. Pedagogiska institutionen, Stockholms universitet. Edsbruk: Akademitryck.

Copley, B., & Forryan, B. (1987). *Therapeutic Work with Children and Young People.* London: Robert Royce.

Coppolillo, H. (1987). *Psychodynamic Psychotherapy of Children. An Introduction to the Art and the Techniques.* Madison, NY: International Universities Press.

Danielson, A. (1998). *Building Your Own World. Manual for the Erica Method.* Stockholm: PsykologiFörlaget.

Edvardson, G. (1985). Barn i sorg, barn i kris. Hjälp till bearbetning genom korttidsterapi. Lund: Natur & Kultur.

Finger, G. (1998). Mit Kindern trauern. Zürich: Kreuz Verlag.

Furman, E. (1986). When is the death of a parent traumatic? *The Psychoanalytic Study of the Child,* XXV, 191–208.

Harding, G. (1969). Leken som avslöjar. Orientering i lekdiagnostik. Stockholm: Natur & Kultur.

Havnesköld, L., & Risholm Mothander, P. (2002). *Utvecklingspsykologi. Psykodynamisk teori i nya perspektiv.* Stockholm: Liber Utbildning.

Haworth, M. (Ed.) (1964.) *Child Psychotherapy. Practice and Theory.* New York: Basic Books.

Haworth, M. (1989). *A Child's Therapy: Hour by Hour.* Madison, NY: International Universities Press.

Jokipaltio, L.-M., Lyytikäinen, K., & Valtonen, H. (Eds.) (1989). *Psykoterapi för barn.* Stockholm: Norstedts förlag.

Karlsson, E. (1977). Barn och sorg. En studie kring sorgearbete under barndomen. Stockholm: Natur & Kultur.

Lantzourakis, A. (1995). *Barnpsykoterapeutisk metodik—några infallsvinklar.* Svenska föreningen för psykisk hälsovård, monografiserie, no. 40.

Lanyado, M., & Horne, A. (1999). *The Handbook of Child & Adolescent Psychotherapy. Psychoanalytic Approaches.* London: Routledge.

Mann, J. (1980). *Tidsbegränsad psykoterapi. En korttidsterapeutisk modell.* Stockholm: Wahlström & Widstrand.

Meyer, W., & Wydler, G. (1986). *Anja. Abenteuer einer Kindertherapie.* Frankfurt am Main: Fischer Verlag.

Moran, G. S. (Ed.) (1987). Some functions of play and playfulness: a developmental perspective. *Psychoanalytic Study of the Child, 42:* 11–29.

Morgan, A. (Ed.) (1999). *Once Upon a Time. Narrative Therapy with Children and their Families.* Adelaide: Dulwich Centre Publications.

Nagera, H. (1970). Children's reactions to the death of important objects. A developmental approach. *The Psychoanalytic Study of the Child, XXV,* 360—400.

Nielsen, G. (1992). Individuell korttids dynamisk psykoterapi med barn: En for lite påaktet arbeidsmåte? *Tidskrift for Norsk Psykologforening, 29,* 428–437.

Nilsson, W. (1997). "Det tar mycket längre tid än man fattar, begriper och förstår ...". En studie av behandlingsarbetet med tidigt kontaktstörda barn ur barnpsykoterapeutens perspektiv. Ericastiftelsen. Rapport nr 9.

Olofgörs, B., & Sjöström, U. (1974). *Barnpsykoterapi.* Lund: Studentlitteratur.

Osofsky, J. D., Cohen, G., & Drell, M. (1995). The effects of trauma on young children: a case of a 2-year-old-twins. *International Journal of Psychoanalysis, 76:* 595–607.

Piovano, B. (1998). *Parallell Psychotherapy with Children and Parents*. New York: Aronson.

Proskauer, S. (1969). Some technical issues in time-limited psychotherapy with children. *Journal of the American Academy of Child Psychiatry, 8*: 154–169.

Rustin, M., & Quagliata, E. (Eds.) (2000). *Assessment in Child Psychotherapy*. London: Duckworth.

Socialdepartementet (1998). Det gäller livet. Stöd och vård till barn och ungdomar med psykiska problem. *Statens offentliga utredningar, 31.*

Stern, D. N. (2000). *The Interpersonal World of the Infant: A View from Psychoanalysis and Developmental Psychology*. New York: Basic Books.

Sylvander, I. (1978). *Barnpsykoterapi*. Stockholm: Natur & Kultur.

Tsiantis, J., Boalt Boëthius, S., Hallerfors, B., Horne, A., & Tischler, L. (Eds.) (2000). *Work with Parents. Psychoanalytic Psychotherapy with Children and Adolescents*. EFPP monograph. London: Karnac.

Tudor-Sandahl, P. (1997). *Ordet är ditt*. Stockholm: Wahlström & Widstrand.

Tydén, A. (2002). Tidsbegränsad barnpsykoterapi - barns och föräldrars erfarenheter. Stockholms läns landsting. Barn- och ungdomspsykiatri, FoU-rapport 02-01.

Vaughn Heineman, T. (2000). Beginning to say goodbye: A two-year-old confronts the death of his father. *Journal of Infant, Child and Adolescent Psychotherapy, 1*(2): 1–22.

Winnicott, D. W. (2005). *Playing and Reality*. London: Routledge.

Wrangsjö, B. (1997). Mötas och växa. Reflexioner kring psykoterapeutyrket. Stockholm: Natur & Kultur.

Books for children

Åkerblom, G. (1996). *Ängel i snön*. Falun: Scandbook AB.

Åkerhielm, H. (1999). *Victorias bönbok*. Stockholm: Hovförsamlingen och Norstedt.

Allan, N. (1996). *Resan dit upp*. Stockholm: Sjöstrands Förlag.

Gripe, M. (1991). *Hugo*. Stockholm: Bonnier.

Lindgren, A. (2000). *Bröderna Lejonhjärta*. Stockholm: Rabén & Sjögren.

Lindgren, A. (2000). *Mio min Mio*. Stockholm: Rabén & Sjögren.

Lindgren, A. (2001). *Pippi Långstrump*. Stockholm: Rabén & Sjögren.

Lindquist, M. (1969). *Malena och glädjen*. Stockholm: Albert Bonniers Boktryckeri.

Lundqvist, A., & Eidem, S. (1992). *Knutte far till himlen*. Stockholm: Natur & Kultur.

Mellonie, B., & Ingpen, R. (1991). *Livet, dess början och slut*. Melbourn: Opal.

Pohl, P., Gieth, K. (1997). *Jag saknar dig, jag saknar dig*. Stockholm: Rabén & Sjögren.

Pohl, P. (1997). *Men jag glömmer dig inte*. Stockholm: Rabén & Sjögren.

Pohl, P. (1999). *Man kan inte säga allt*. Stockholm: Rabén & Sjögren.

Stalfelt, P. (1999). *Döden boken*. Eriksson & Lindgren.

Stark, U., & Höglund, A. (1995). *Liten*. Stockholm: Alfabeta Bokförlag.

Stark, U., & Höglund, A. (1996). *Min syster är en ängel*. Stockholm: Alfabeta Bokförlag.

Stark, U., & Höglund, A. (1997). *Ängeln och den blåa hästen*. Stockholm: Alfabeta Bokförlag.

Stark, U., & Höglund, A. (1998). *Lilla Asmodeus*. Stockholm: Alfabeta Bokförlag.

Stark, U., & Höglund, A. (2000). *Den svarta fiolen*. Stockholm: Alfabeta Bokförlag.

Sundvall, V. (1993). *Bland fimpar och rosor*. Stockholm: Rabén & Sjögren.

Thun, M. (1991). *Ängelungen*. Finland: WSOY.

Tidholm, T., & Tidholm, A.-C. (1987). *Resan till Ugri-La-Brek*. Stockholm: Alfabeta Bokförlag.

Velthuijs, M. (1991). *Grodan och fågelsången*. Stockholm: Berghs Förlag.

Warrebäck, R. M. (1995). *Robbans bok om när pappa dog*. Stockholm: Proprius Förlag.

Wollnick, T. (1996). *Torsken och döden*. Stockholm: Norstedts Förlag.

INDEX